Bringing **Maths** and **English** together across the curriculum

Lisa Jane Ashes

@lisajaneashes

First published by

Independent Thinking Press

Crown Buildings, Bancyfelin, Carmarthen, Wales, SA33 5ND, UK

www.independentthinkingpress.com

Independent Thinking Press is an imprint of Crown House Publishing Ltd.

Photograph page 1 © Emma Tuck

Illustration page 114 © ruddall30, fotolia.com

British Library of Cataloguing-in-Publication Data

A catalogue entry for this book is available from the British Library.

Print ISBN: 9781781351017
Mobi ISBN: 9781781351420
ePub ISBN: 9781781351437
ePDF ISBN: 9781781351444

Printed and bound in the UK by
Stephens and George, Dowlais, Merthyr Tydfil

For the love, sparkles, rainbows, empty mugs, tough love, direction, babysitting, tea, books, ideas, push, belief, opportunity and inspiration.

This is for you.

CONTENTS

ACKNOWLEDGEMENTS

I wish to express my great appreciation to Jane Hutchison for her role in the development of GAP SPLITT. To Gary Mitchelson, I extend my sincere thanks for his collaboration in the creation of Joseph Swan Academy's Key Stage 3 curriculum. Without these two colleagues, Manglish may never have been born.

I would like to acknowledge all those colleagues, both present and past, from Joseph Swan and those who collaborated from far and wide, who supported me though discussion of Manglish ideas, practised Manglish in their classrooms or schools and provided me with feedback to move forward.

Special thanks must go to my husband, Tony Ashes. His Manglish mind has been the inspiration behind all of my ideas – and his meals have kept me alive.

PROLOGUE

A taste of the future

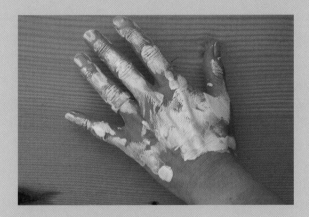

Where's the maths in that?

Look at the image above and ask yourself: where's the maths in that?

Recently, I put the same question and image to a group of Scottish teachers in Edinburgh. To find the answer, they needed to interrogate the image further. I used question balls to get them going.[1] The teachers picked

---

1   A question ball is simply a plastic ball with a question stem written on it which is placed into a mini ball pool.

out one ball at a time and created their own questions about the possibilities for maths in the image. Modern technology has not come on far enough to allow me to integrate an actual ball pool into this book. Instead, I have provided you with some visual examples of the balls so you can have a go yourself. Using one ball at a time, look again at the picture. Complete the stem and create a question that helps you further investigate the possibility of maths being contained in the image.

Here are some of the questions that my Scottish friends asked that day:

> What is the white stuff?
> Did the white stuff get there because they were cooking?
> Where was this picture taken?
> Could this person be a skilled craftsperson?
> Why is Lisa asking us to find the maths in a random image?

After a few minutes, the teachers were slowing down in their discussion – a *boom* moment was required. They had determined that there definitely was potential to find maths in the image, but it was time to get more precise with what maths was actually there.

I began throwing thought bombs to provoke new thinking and a more focused discussion.[2] As technology has come no further since page one, you will once again have to make do with an image to represent the thoughts being thrown.

---

2   A thought bomb is simply a dressed-up ball which is painted black, has a string fuse and is sprinkled with glitter. It has a hole in the bottom for the insertion of new ideas, which can be written on slips of paper and inserted into the bomb to help explode the thoughts that are already being formed. The idea for thought bombs came from reading Hywel Roberts's book *Oops!* (Carmarthen: Independent Thinking Press, 2012), in which he describes throwing thought grenades at children to explode their thinking. Awesome book!

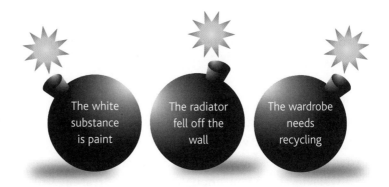

The teachers began reorganising their ideas based on what was contained in the bombs. The cooking idea was quickly thrown out and new ideas were added in its place. Once the teachers had begun forming an extensive list of the potential maths contained in the image (we were only about five minutes into the session here – it wasn't difficult), I provided them with a brief overview of the key concepts and processes teachers are expected to draw on when teaching mathematics in schools:

Number and algebra

Rational numbers, their properties and their different representations; rules of arithmetic applied to calculations and manipulations with rational numbers; applications of ratio and proportion; accuracy and rounding; algebra as generalised arithmetic; linear equations, formulae, expressions and identities; analytical, graphical and numerical methods for solving equations; polynomial graphs, sequences and functions; experimental and theoretical probabilities.

Geometry and measures

Properties of 2D and 3D shapes; constructions, loci and bearings; Pythagoras' theorem; transformations; similarity, including the use of scale; points, lines and shapes in 2D coordinate systems; units, compound measures and conversions; perimeters, areas, surface areas and volumes.

Statistics

The handling data cycle; presentation and analysis of grouped and ungrouped data, including time series and lines of best fit; measures of central tendency and spread; experimental and theoretical probabilities, including those based on equally likely outcomes.[3]

I asked the teachers to start linking the maths they had suggested may be in the image with the maths currently being taught to pupils in Key Stage 3. Have a go at doing the same thing with your own ideas – look at the maths you have found in your investigations and try to see how much of the maths taught at Key Stage 3 was relevant to your thoughts about this real-life situation.

The Scottish teachers began making links such as:

> Having knowledge of perimeters and areas could help you fit an old wardrobe safely into the car on the way to the tip.

> Understanding the rules of arithmetic could help you add up totals quickly when calculating the correct position to reattach the radiator.

Every teacher, no matter what their specialist subject, agreed that the maths being taught had a real purpose beyond the maths lesson.

Next came the revelation of the actual source of the image. A day earlier, my husband and I had been decorating. I watched in awe as he transformed an old wardrobe into a brand new shelving unit (using his knowledge of geometry and measures); a radiator fell off and he refitted it in a more suitable place (using his knowledge of numbers and calculation); he plastered our whole bedroom, buying the correct amount of plaster (numbers and calculation) and mixing suitable quantities (ratio and proportion) to help him to avoid wastage. The room was transformed at minimal cost and with maximum aesthetic effect. My only job in all of this was to buy the paint.

As I left my home to travel to the Edinburgh Libraries Pedagoo TeachMeet, the room I left behind was only half finished. Not because I didn't have time but because I didn't buy nearly enough paint.

Maths is in everything. It is one of the most purposeful and applicable

---

3   Department for Education, Mathematics: Range and Content (2 August 2013). Available at: <http://www.education.gov.uk/schools/teachingandlearning/curriculum/secondary/b00199003/mathematics/ks3/programme/range>.

subjects on the curriculum; we use it every day in our adult lives. My lack of ability to apply maths in everyday life originates from my lack of ability to see a point in maths at school – which, of course, has had unfortunate consequences in later life. After driving to the shops, I looked at a tin of paint that appeared to be large enough to cover the room (missing the point of calculation and area). The idea that I could have used the actual dimensions of the room and read the coverage instructions on the tin to work out what size tin would be most cost effective never crossed my mind. When I arrived home, I held my proud purchase up to my husband's unimpressed face. It took him only a few seconds to apply his understanding of accurate estimation and probability to work out that the tin was much too small. Ultimately, my lack of ability to apply maths in this real-life context wound up costing us time and money. Thank goodness I can spell.

Manglish was an idea born from my disjointed experiences at school. Never entering a maths class again meant to me that maths was over; I never needed to think about that subject again (until the next time I reluctantly arrived in that part of the school again). Similarly, the perfectly polished essays that I created in my English lessons were not replicated in written reports for subjects such as geography or art. I just could not see the link. Manglish is a way of organising the curriculum collaboratively to create openings for cross-curricular links. It provides pupils with purposeful opportunities to explore how applicable maths, reading, writing and communication can be in other subject areas and the wider world.

Departments beginning their Manglish journey – particularly those subjects that do not have an obvious connection to skills such as reading, writing, communication and maths – will need to go through a process of questioning similar to the questions asked by the Scottish teachers above. Teachers must see for themselves the opportunities for maths, reading, writing and communication that already exist in their subject areas and understand that these opportunities can be made obvious and purposeful for their pupils. They must ask themselves, where is the maths in my subject? Where are the communication, reading and writing opportunities that already exist and how can we work together to create a more joined-up approach to supporting pupils who are learning to master them?

We have looked at an image which, on first glance, appears to have no connection whatsoever with maths; we could do the same for reading, writing and communication. Think of that image as your subject as you begin your Manglish planning. Question it and see for yourself how your subject has enormous potential for requiring your pupils to have an understanding of these four essential skills.

Mathematics and communication

The term Manglish was a nickname that stuck. The idea came when my school, Joseph Swan Academy, decided to reform its Key Stage 3 curriculum. Gary Mitchelson (the maths AST) and I were the driving force behind the changes. We were tasked with creating a purposeful and engaging Key Stage 3 curriculum, which covered all of the usual acronyms provided by the introduction of new Ofsted criteria. RWCM (reading, writing, communication and mathematics) was just one of them. We collaborated with departments to raise expectations and develop opportunities for mathematics, reading, writing and communication skills to be applied across the curriculum. We developed methods of differentiation that teachers could put into action to create consistency for pupils. Following the creation of this curriculum, we stayed in contact with our link departments and ensured that the skills developed during planning were being followed through into lessons. We supported teachers when they had difficulties in making links and observed many successes as a result of our major overhaul.

Manglish has since evolved into a way of creating a secondary school curriculum that allows pupils to experience reading, writing, communication and maths purposefully in *every* lesson. The pages that follow will take you through the steps required to create your own Manglish curriculum from scratch. If you are looking for tips to support reading, writing, communication and maths, you will find examples of Manglish lessons in action, along with supporting materials in the form of Manglish mats and simple GAP SPLITT planning guides. Manglish mats are criteria adapted from reading, writing, communication and mathematics levels and are used to support all teachers in understanding pupils' working-at levels and in developing lessons with effective use of differentiation. GAP SPLITT guides are for pupil use and are a cross-curricular planning mat used specifically for writing.

The following chapters will take you through how to create the curriculum, use the resources and explore many different ways of collaborating. You will be exploring, not because the Ofsted inspector is coming and the school suddenly needs to show willing in supporting maths and English teachers with literacy and numeracy, but because pupils need to *see* how reading, writing, communication and mathematics can be applied in real contexts. In doing so, pupils are able to experience how effective communication can help them to become successful – for example, to understand how their recently acquired knowledge of space and shape can support them to create ergonomically effective products in design and technology. Not accidentally, but because the opportunities have been recognised and purposefully built in. The Manglish curriculum provides opportunities to build upon what is being explicitly taught in English and maths lessons; opportunities to practise literacy and numeracy skills are understood and acted upon. Pupils experiencing the Manglish curriculum should feel that there is a point to everything they learn and no new learning is left behind in an individual classroom but is taken forward, used and improved. No matter which road pupils take in life, they will have experienced an education that has taught them the importance of joined-up thinking.

Pupils like me, the ones who spend their time asking 'What's the point?', are not just looking to disrupt, they are searching for a 'why?' Why are you making their head hurt with all of this difficult new information? Why should they keep listening when it is so difficult to grasp? A pupil experiencing the Manglish curriculum should be able to tell the teacher why. The perfect end product will not only be a knowledgeable pupil but one who is able to practise their skills with autonomy. Autonomous pupils know that what they are learning is transferable and will be used as they journey through their other lessons and through life. Rather than asking 'What's the point?', the Manglish pupil will be bursting to tell you what they did with last week's mathematical learning in geography. As pupils undertake research into characterisation in English, they will impress the teacher with their ability to use statistics (covered during the previous half-term) to effectively to support their investigations. Joined-up thinking will run through their veins. The architects born of a Manglish curriculum will take inspiration from historical events; the artists will use ratios effectively to produce artworks filled with beauty; the scientists will think creatively about new avenues of research by drawing on their ability to analyse and question; and they will all live economically as a result of their ability to effectively apply numerical skill.

The Manglish curriculum provides pupils with clarity and support, tailored to their individual needs. As they leave their primary experience behind and enter the world of secondary school, where each subject is taught discretely by different teachers, they are still able to see that links between their learning experience in one subject can explicitly relate to their experience in another. They will see that teachers are working together to support each other in the creation of the perfect final product; no opportunities are missed and no child gets left behind. The final product of a Manglish curriculum is a whole child, one who is independent, able to communicate effectively and use a range of skills to engage with the adult world of learning, which is about to open up to them. The Manglish child is not just a bag of bits – they are a complete and effective learner, primed for a successful future.

Developing a Manglish curriculum will help everyone, pupils and teachers alike, to make links between all learning in order to become highly literate and numerate citizens. Maths teachers who develop a Manglish state of mind will not only teach pupils mathematics, they will also develop lessons that support pupils in becoming effective communicators – as in the example described below.[4]

Teachers of mathematics in a Manglish school know, thanks to collaborative planning and the central data provided by English teachers, that pupils have been focusing on, for example, communication during English lessons. This central system should also provide teachers with pupils' working-at levels so that teachers can plan to support pupils in their progression. Manglish

---

4   This lesson has been adapted from Lisa Jane Ashes, No Pens Day, *Reflections of a Learning Geek* (29 August 2013). Available at: <http://thelearninggeek.com/2013/08/no-pens-day/>.

mats are resources developed by the school to create consistency in teachers' understanding of what pupils' working-at levels actually mean in practice. They are called mats, rather than tables, because they should be physical mats that teachers lay out in front of them as they plan lessons, enabling them to differentiate for individual needs. Example mats and ideas for differentiation are provided in this book, but mats that are produced by individual schools will be far more effective because teachers will have collaborated to create mats that make sense to them.

Teachers of English have, using the coloured system on the Manglish mats, recorded pupils in this class as having a current working-at level of **Blue Silver** and they are all working towards **Blue Gold** communication. This system of red mats for higher-ability pupils and blue for lower-ability pupils allows teachers to differentiate without looking at every level of the criteria at once. These mats are then further divided into gold, silver and bronze – six levels in total. Note that all teachers in the school are using the same mats and criteria for reading, writing, communication and maths. You will be shown exactly how to do this for yourself very soon.

In maths, pupils are discovering the language associated with angles and are working towards **Blue Gold** in their term-specific mathematics, which this half-term is geometry and measures. At the end of the lesson, the teacher has gathered written evidence that pupils can write down the appropriate mathematical language associated with angles and use it correctly, but now wants to review this to ensure all pupils have fully understood (and not just copied from a friend). In order to undertake a review, the teacher sets up peer teaching pairs, where one pupil is given five minutes to discuss what they have discovered about angles before the other takes over and does the same.

As the teacher circulates the room, they listen for understanding of the topic, while also encouraging pupils to achieve success in their ability to present their ideas to one another. This will not only support their learning in English but it will also encourage them to give better quality explanations which the teacher can listen to for both understanding and any misconceptions. Pupils are being shown that effective communication is applicable beyond the English classroom and has a real purpose.

The teacher has given them the following bullet points, adapted from her Manglish mats, to aid them in their success:

> Make sure you explain your findings clearly – your listener must understand.
> Try to be interesting in your delivery to hold your listener's attention.
> Could you use examples, images or gestures?

As the teacher circulates, she hears the following comment from a pupil: 'I learned that there are lots of angles. I learned their names and what they do.' The pupil is not making eye contact and is instead looking in his book to remind himself of his work. The pupil is recounting this experience in a very simple way. He is only holding the attention of his listener because he has been partnered up with his best friend.

The teacher knows that the pupil is at least capable of **Blue Silver** communication and is therefore not recognising that the skills learned this term in English are also applicable here. The teacher is able to ask the pupil to review his success criteria, adapted from the Manglish mat, to achieve better quality communication and demonstrate a higher level of mathematical understanding.

Reminded of his lessons in English this week, the pupil realises he must attempt to use detail and vocabulary choices that are matched to his listener. He adapts his response using his criteria as a guide and, as the teacher leaves him to listen in to other conversations, she hears the pupil say (making eye contact with his partner): 'Today, the most interesting angle I have discovered is the acute angle, an angle between 0 and 90 degrees [he draws an example to demonstrate what this would look like]. I really like that the name of this angle helps me to remember that it is small.'

This is not literacy and numeracy across the curriculum simply to tick an Ofsted box. This is a school that is very aware of the learning in which each child is taking part. The mathematics teacher is aware of what good communication looks and sounds like, thanks to collaborative planning and the help of the Manglish mat as a guide. The teacher did not have to change the content of his lesson, but instead used this knowledge to change how the lesson was reviewed.

Do you want to see this in your school? Let's get planning!

1 Starting from scratch

Why we need a blank slate

To create the perfect Manglish curriculum, all staff members will need to be prepared to start from scratch. The whole school should be on board and a brave head teacher will need to invest time and effort in its creation. However, if you are merely one person and you are not yet in a powerful enough position to make that happen, do not stop reading! You can still use this book to make a difference for your pupils. The ideas contained in each section will allow you to develop Manglish experiences within individual lessons. A lone teacher can make a difference to a number of pupils; however, if a whole-school approach is adopted, we can change the attitudes of whole generations. If whole countries were to adopt a more joined-up approach to teaching, then we could change the economic future of the world!

Before the national curriculum (which was introduced in England, Wales and Northern Ireland as part of the Education Reform Act 1988), experience of a range of subjects did not come as a right for all pupils, which frequently left the poorest in society at a disadvantage. Secondary schools now give all children access to knowledge about the history of their country and the opportunity to learn foreign languages and to play a musical instrument.

This is great, but it has also left teachers of individual subjects isolated from one another. Subject specialists are compartmentalised and pupils rarely see for themselves how the knowledge acquired in one subject can be applicable in another. Pupils might spend an hour learning to understand space and shape in a design and technology lesson, but do not go on and employ the principles learned (even though the opportunity could easily have been built in). These links must be made explicit to young people.

The example Manglish curriculum outlined in this book would be suitable for delivering to a Year 7 cohort in England. In theory, you could just copy everything and practise it verbatim; however, that's not really the point. For one thing, curriculums change as subjects are added or taken away at the whim of government. You need to engage with Manglish as a state of mind if you are going to really make it work. To get *your* Manglish curriculum right, *you* will need to start from scratch with *your* school and *your* pupils' needs in mind. If you adopt Manglish as a mindset, you are no longer thinking within subject areas but as a whole school. As a whole school, you will adapt to any new expectations that are thrown at you and work together with the pupils' future needs at the heart of your plans.

I am about to take you step by step through the Manglish planning process to show you how you can create a similar approach in your school. The core planning begins with English and maths teachers, but the aim is to develop a curriculum with colleagues from all departments. In turn, this will create pupils and educators who see and apply links between all learning.

What do *your* pupils need to know?

We may be starting from scratch but we aren't throwing everything out of the window. We all know that we can't teach just any old thing to our pupils; there are certain expectations for schools set out in government policies that tie our hands, and most of this already exists in the national curriculum. We must cover our backs and make sure we teach everything we are told to teach – but that doesn't mean we all have to teach it in the same way.

To plan the basic overview for your Manglish curriculum, you must start with a blank canvas and create a shopping list for teaching English and maths that covers all the necessary programmes of study and attainment targets. For example, Joseph Swan Academy is following an English curriculum that states the following must be taught: speaking and listening, spoken language, other cultures, extended reading, plays, Shakespeare, poetry and writing for various purposes. The mathematics curriculum states that pupils must cover: numbers, algebra, calculation, statistics, probability, geometry, measures, ratio, proportion and rates of change. Within each of these topics, there are many layers of skill which must also be taught, so skills are also fully audited at this time and put onto our shopping lists. This information will be useful later during the creation of the Manglish mats. (A more detailed explanation of the Manglish mat is set out at the end of this chapter and examples of completed mats can be found on pages 32–43.)

This part of the process requires the collaboration of every member of the English and maths departments. Pupils need consistency and, at this point in the development of our own curriculum, we found that English and maths teachers were not consistent in their approach to topics. There is nothing wrong with teaching in your own style, but when pupils have to learn different methods for multiplication or develop a new approach to written plans just because that's how their new teacher prefers to do it, essential time is being wasted.

Typically, a student will have a new teacher for English and maths every year in their lower schooling, meaning that they may have changed their way of approaching a topic – particularly a method that already works for them – up to three times. Pupils may also be unlucky enough to have a split timetable and may be asked to approach the same topic using two different methods at any one time – confusing! Once a pupil becomes highly skilled at a topic, there is plenty of merit in demonstrating various styles of approach – the pupil can then choose the most effective method for them. However, this should be included as differentiation for such pupils, rather than causing confusion and losing precious learning time for the masses.

Once the shopping list for exactly what is going to be taught is complete, the English and maths departments can then create the order in which the topics would best be taught. For example:

Half-term	Mathematics	English
1	Numbers/calculation/algebra	Writing for purpose and audience: fiction (Shakespeare/poetry)
2	Statistics/probability	Reading for meaning
3	Geometry/measures	Spoken language/speaking and listening
4	Ratio/proportion/rates of change	Writing for purpose and audience: non-fiction
5	Probability/statistics 2	Reading for meaning (plays/ autobiography)
6	Review	Review

Making purposeful links

Once the maths and English departments have their solid plan for the year in place, the other departments are now ready to do the same. However, as English and maths are the driving force behind the Manglish curriculum, their job is not yet complete. During the reformation of Joseph Swan Academy's curriculum, all departments were led through the same process of plotting out their own subjects' needs and expectations by myself and our maths AST, Gary Mitchelson.

Teachers didn't scrap their topics in favour of teaching English and maths; however, they did ensure that what was being taught was engaging, relevant and purposeful. As literacy and numeracy provide the foundations for all other learning, opportunities for developing these skills exist in all subjects (even if they are not immediately obvious). Gary and I were there to support teachers in finding the openings that already existed within their subjects. Where is the maths in that, Mr Historian? Where is the opportunity for communication, Mrs Physics? Where are you already practising reading skills, Mr Geographer? What purposes do you need to write for, Mrs Music?

We were not there to force our own subjects into theirs, but to explore where the skills already exist. Remember, there is maths in everything, but you must make that maths explicit, real and applicable if you are going to support your pupils in seeing its purpose and embedding that skill for life.

Once you have completed the collaboration between departments, your skeleton plan should now resemble something like this:

Half-term	Mathematics	English	Linking to:
1	Numbers/ calculation/ algebra	Writing for purpose and audience 1: fiction (Shakespeare/ poetry)	**History:** Europe and the wider world, 1901 to present day **Technology:** design, make, evaluate, technical knowledge
2	Statistics/ probability	Reading for meaning 1	**Citizenship:** civil liberties and the law **Science:** biology, genetics and evolution
3	Geometry/ measures	Spoken language/ speaking and listening	**MFL:** manipulating key grammatical structures including voices and moods
4	Ratio/proportion/ rates of change	Writing for purpose and audience: non-fiction	**Music:** improvise and compose **Computing:** creative project to select, use and combine multiple applications
5	Probability/ statistics 2	Reading for meaning (plays/ autobiography)	**Geography:** human and physical geography **PE:** developing physical techniques
6	Review	Review	Review

This table represents a basic overview, demonstrating which subjects will be collaborating at which times. As a result of detailed conversations at a subject and departmental level during the planning process, individual subject teachers should also come away with extensive lists of what each of their half-terms will contain in terms of content, progression and skills. Consequently, each department in your school has a plan for the year ahead. In theory, they could return to school and practise what they have set out with success, but don't forget that continuing collaboration is absolutely essential. Teachers need to plan not only individual learning experiences together, but also to review these experiences regularly to assess their purpose and effect.

Imagine that this plan was created collaboratively, but then the lead teachers from English and maths and the teachers delivering the skills in other subjects never meet again. Teachers experiencing success may flourish; they may make links and develop reading, writing, communication and maths all by themselves. But without effective communication between departments, links may still be lost on the pupils as, for example, their learning in English is, for one reason or another, no longer progressing according to the plan. Similarly, teachers who struggle will soon scrap the new ideas in favour of tried and tested approaches to their own subjects, perhaps fearing examination failure. The key to success is continuing evaluation, discussion, ideas and support when things do not go to plan.

Dedicating time to this process is crucial. Teachers are overworked – fact! The initial planning is hard work, but it will pay off in time as a smarter way of working evolves. Effective planning will mean that collaborating teachers will begin to share workloads – for example, teachers of English will be marking homework tasks for teachers of PE. This should not mean that teachers of English take on *extra* marking (goodness only knows, they have enough already). Rather, English teachers' homework, which would usually be set by them, is set by PE that week. The English teachers then use this to inform their planning of pupil progression as they would have done with their own set homework. Similarly, teachers of maths won't need to set homework this week because the geography department has set a task for them. Teachers of both departments will then work together to analyse the results – all teachers are working together towards a common goal of pupil progress. We will look at how this works in practice in more detailed lesson planning on pages 24–26, but understand that time set aside for collaborative planning is essential.

Big ideas and relevant learning

All teachers should be aware of the bigger picture, whether it is their collaborative half-term (i.e. the half-term that they are linked to the English and maths departments, as in the table above) or not. Likewise, all teachers should be aware of the importance of making connections between learning experiences. The Manglish curriculum teaches pupils about the importance of making connections between everything, and so adopts a more 'expert' approach to learning. Industry experts may specialise in one area but they are always able to draw on their knowledge of other subject areas when necessary. In contrast, pupils often do not see how their mathematical knowledge can support them in their geographical studies, or how essay planning in English will be valuable to them in their PE written exam. If they aspire to a more integrated way of working, they will become more adept at selecting appropriate cross-curricular skills and therefore begin to act more like the experts they aspire to be.

Once departments become more confident with the application of reading, writing, communication and mathematics, following their collaborative half-term, they should begin to recognise opportunities to make links for themselves between the learning across the curriculum. After a few years of practising the Manglish approach, you will have teachers who are expert in finding opportunities to collaborate, not because they are told to but because they have experienced the success that working together towards a common purpose creates.

By following the process outlined above, your Manglish curriculum now has an effective skeleton structure. All subjects have been linked to maths and English and subject teachers have been coached in seeing for themselves the opportunities that exist to sustain effective collaboration and the application of skills from one subject to the next. Each half-term will now be given a 'big idea' as a driving force behind the collaboration taking place. The big idea should engage pupils and give teachers a planning focus that can span the whole curriculum. This big idea must be abstract enough to encompass every subject and allow interesting content to be developed from it. For example, if the big idea were Shakespeare, then it would be far too subject specific. Maths teachers would be turned off and it is hard to see what tenuous links would have to be made to get the idea into design and technology (Shakespeare music boxes perhaps?). Similarly, if bridges were the big idea, maths teachers might flourish but English teachers would suffer from attempting to teach poems about bridges in an engaging way.

The big idea should be agreed upon by all departments and should make learning relevant for all your pupils. Magic would be my first choice for an initial Year 7 big idea – what child does not enjoy magic? And what a wonderful way to open your first year with these pupils, still fresh and enthusiastic from primary school, where it is still seen as acceptable to stick your hand up to answer every question. In mathematics, the idea that you can perform magic with numbers, as long as you learn how they work, is a far more engaging way to teach the number system than endless abstract and seemingly inapplicable sums. In English, pupils can learn about the illusion of writing and the writer as a magical being – someone who can create a whole new world from their imagination. In design and technology, the magical enthusiasm can continue into artistic creations which are mathematical in design but full of creativity. Did you know that magicians played an integral part in the success of two world wars? No? Well, pupils studying history will as this engaging big idea continues.

It is essential to have continuity across the curriculum, and a thematic approach to curriculum planning can support pupils when they are making links between learning. However, the big idea is merely the tip of the iceberg – the Manglish curriculum represents far more than just a theme.

Manglish is not a content-empty plan; on the contrary, engaging and cultural content is an integral part of its success. Pupils will find out about their ancestors, the origins of ideas, the wonder of cultural identity and what it really means to be a citizen of our world. In English lessons, pupils should be allowed to critically explore a myriad of writers and contexts both modern and historic; they should use this inspiration to experiment with their own personal writing styles. Pupils should be writing for contexts beyond their own classroom and understanding the contemporary world around them. I am sure that this is the aim of any curriculum plan. Where Manglish is different, however, is in the links made between historical periods being studied in other curriculum areas, such as history and art, to reinforce pupils' knowledge and understanding of national and international cultures. In maths lessons, pupils will engage with problems that develop their understanding of not only famous mathematicians, but also individuals you would not ordinarily associate with mathematics – for example, Harry Houdini, a logical thinker with a creative soul. As a result, the new learning will not be left behind in their mathematics classroom; it will be further developed as collaborative planning has taken place and plans have been created which will allow pupils to explore these great figures in other subject areas. Pupils should be hungry to find out more as each new cultural revelation engages their curiosity.

The table on the following page gives an overview of the way content may be planned collaboratively across the curriculum.

Half-term	Big Idea	Maths content
1	Magic	**Numbers, calculation and algebra** How did Harry Houdini work out his escape every time? Pupils are introduced to the mathematics behind the magic. They are taught to understand rational numbers; rules of arithmetic applied to calculations and manipulations with rational numbers; application of ratio and proportion; accuracy and rounding; algebra as generalised arithmetic; linear equations to recognise solutions; formulaic expressions and identity; analytical, graphical and numerical methods for solving equations; and polynomial graphs, sequences and functions. They use it all to make magic of their own.
2	Big Brother	**Statistics/probability** Pupils will be using their understanding of data to create their own experiments based on famous social experiments. They can use the TV show *Big Brother* as an example or opt to go for older historical experiments. Pupils will be taught to understand how to handle a data cycle using grouped and ungrouped data. They will learn about the presentation of data including lines of best fit; measures of central tendency and spread; range and interquartile range; and experimental and theoretical probabilities. They will learn to predict likely outcomes using frequency analysis and how to record data accurately.
3	Top Teams	**Geometry and measures** Exploring the mathematical skill of the team of engineers that built the Millennium Dome/Millennium Bridge. Pupils will learn about the properties of 3D and 2D shapes, constructions, loci and bearing. They will be taught to use straight-edged compasses and Pythagoras' theorem to perform transformations. They will be exploring the use of scale. Pupils will also look into points, lines and shapes in 2D coordinate systems. They will be using units/compound measures and conversions (e.g. fuel consumption/speed acceleration), perimeters, areas, surface areas and volumes.

English content	Linking to ...
Writing for purpose and audience As a stimulus for their own creative writing, pupils will be studying *A Midsummer Night's Dream*, alongside magical poems and short stories to recognise the writer as an illusionist. Pupils will be taught to plan, draft, edit and proofread. They must learn to consider purpose, audience and reception as well as vocabulary, grammar, structure and spelling. Pupils will be taught to write accurately and fluently at length, drawing on knowledge of vocabulary, grammar, text structures, literary and rhetorical devices.	**History** Pupils are learning how mathematical knowledge won the war. Jasper Maskelyne and illusions during war time. Did ghost armies exist or was it all just an illusion? **Design and technology** Developing illusions in artistic creations. Pupils will use their understanding of creating for specific audiences and purposes to create illusions. Pupils will also use mathematical skill during the construction of their products.
Reading for meaning Pupils will be exploring George Orwell's *1984* and understanding satire and context, and how terms and concepts such as 'Big Brother is watching you' enter the mainstream, using frequency analysis of words and linking the work to mathematics. Pupils will also understand how writers create rounded characters that match their genre, audience and purpose. Pupils will be gathering data from different sources for comparison. Pupils will be learning to use quotations and correctly reference texts.	**Citizenship** The legal system in the UK, CCTV and human rights. Should Big Brother be watching us? **Science – biology, genetics and evolution** Analysis and evaluation of humans as a species. Pupils will be using mathematical concepts, calculating results and identifying further questions based upon new evidence. What makes us human? Using famous experiments to understand and explore further what makes us human.
Spoken language Analysis of spoken language of characters vs. real-life talk – what's the difference? Pupils become a team of investigators to explore spoken language in the world. They will be taking part in formal presentations and debates, using Standard English when appropriate. They will also take on fictional roles to explore ideas. Pupils will be taught to vary their structure and vocabulary according to purpose, listeners, and content; listen and respond to others, including in pairs and groups, shaping meanings through suggestions, comments and questions; create and sustain different roles, adapting dramatic techniques; understand the range and uses of spoken language, commenting on meaning and impact, and draw on this when talking to others.	**MFL** Communication difficulties transcending language barriers. How does speech in another language differ from our own language? Using knowledge of spoken languages to make comparisons. Use of statistics to gather and interpret data.

Half-term	Big Idea	Maths content
4	Going Digital	**Ratio/proportion/rates of change** Looking at the effect of the Internet on business development. Linking to projects in English and computing by exploring up-scaling a website to reach a wider audience. Pupils will learn to use ratio and scale-factor notation as well as methods involving conversion, mixing, measuring and scaling when comparing quantities and concentrations. Pupils will be taught to calculate missing quantities using given ratios; solve problems including percentage change; use multiplicative reasoning where two quantities have a fixed product; use compound units; and solve kinematic problems such as speed.
5	Going for Gold	**Probability/statistics 2** Pupils will be taught to record and describe the frequency of outcomes; enumerate sets and combinations of sets systematically using tables, grids and Venn diagrams; generate theoretical sample spaces and use them to generate theoretical probabilities; describe and compare using appropriate graphical representations and describe relationships between variables.
6	Project X	Inter-department collaborative project

English content	Linking to ...
Writing for audience and purpose Linking with a school from a different cultural background, pupils will be creating an informative website to introduce them to the culture of this school. The preparation for written sections and organisation will take place in English. Pupils will be practising their ability to plan, draft, edit and proofread, considering purpose, audience reception, vocabulary, grammar, structure and spelling. Pupils will be practising their ability to write accurately and fluently at length, drawing on knowledge of vocabulary, grammar, text structures, literary and rhetorical devices.	**Music** Designing effective tracks to enhance their school website with a specific audience in mind. They will be composing the music themselves and deciding where and how it should be used to help other cultures to understand ours. **Computing** Building the website for the audience and purpose set out in English, using an understanding of geometry and measures from last half-term for effective designs, using problem-solving and communication skills to work as a design team in the final production of the product planned in English.
Reading Pupils will be reading and comparing autobiographies/articles on successful people, including local heroes. Pupils will also explore autobiographical poems and plays. Pupils can begin by comparing the biography of Katie Price with that of Nelson Mandela. Pupils should be encouraged to make their own choices following this to encourage their own critical tastes. Pupils will be taught to read critically to know how language, form, vocabulary choice and structure inform meaning, and recognise differences in language use when comparing different texts.	**Geography** The reason for country rankings. Why is Britain not number one in the world? Pupils will be gathering data about a number of countries and presenting their findings in a written report for the government, describing the improvements to be made based on their findings. **PE** Using self-gathered data to improve physical skills and be the best that you can possibly be. The practical ideas developed during lesson time will be further explored in mathematical and written homework tasks that support the learning in lessons. English and mathematics teachers should collaborate with PE teachers on the homework tasks as they may be followed up in English and mathematics lessons to support progression.
Inter-department collaborative project	Inter-department collaborative project

Collaboration

As the curriculum is being planned collaboratively, and teachers of all subjects are supported in their planning by English and maths specialists, opportunities to review and use reading, writing, communication and mathematical skills should no longer be missed. Manglish supports not only the development of effective learners but also the up-skilling of teachers through teamwork.

Teachers should not fear English and maths if they intend to cultivate pupils who leave school confident with their ability to apply literacy and numeracy skills in any context. All teachers, not just maths and English teachers, have an important role to play in changing the negative attitudes of young people.[1] How many times have you heard a well-educated colleague say, 'I'm no good at maths' or 'I'm terrible at spelling'? Pupils, in turn, feel that it is acceptable to be 'bad at maths' or 'rubbish at spelling', and so the legacy continues into the next generation.

The Manglish curriculum will not only develop highly skilled pupils but it will also have the exponential effect of creating highly skilled and creative teachers who see the applicability of, and links between, learning. Teachers who model positive attitudes towards the use of these important literacy and numeracy skills will have a more positive effect on pupils' attitudes. The end result will be a generation of pupils willing and able to use maths and English in a range of contexts – an employer's dream cohort.

Once departments have completed their collaborative half-term with the English and maths departments, they should be given the opportunity to share their experiences and successes with other departments and support colleagues in identifying further opportunities for reading, writing, communication and maths. Therefore, beginning in half-term 2, departments should be paired up with each other as lead teams and developing teams. The lead team will have just completed their Manglish unit and should share their good practice. They should demonstrate how they used the Manglish mat

---

1   Much research has gone into the effects of negative attitudes towards maths. You can read more about this on the National Numeracy website: <http://www.nationalnumeracy.org.uk/campaigning-changing-attitudes/index.html>.

Half-term	Big Idea	Maths content	English content	Linking to ...	Best practice sharing
1	**Magic**	Numbers, calculation and algebra	Writing for purpose and audience 1: fiction	History Design and technology	
2	**Big Brother**	Statistics/probability	Reading for meaning	Citizenship Science	**Leading team** History Design and technology **Developing team** Art Music
3	**Top Teams**	Geometry and measures	Spoken language	MFL	**Leading team** Citizenship Science **Developing team** Computing Design and technology
4	**Going Digital**	Ratio/proportion/rates of change	Writing for audience and purpose 2: non-fiction	Music Computing	**Leading team** MFL **Developing team** Science Citizenship
5	**Going for Gold**	Probability/statistics 2	Reading	Geography PE	**Leading team** Music Computing **Developing team** MFL
6	**Project X**	Inter-department collaborative project	Inter-department collaborative project	Inter-department collaborative project	Inter-department collaborative project

to identify opportunities and support pupils in applying practical skills in their context. The developing team should then be guided by the lead team in identifying opportunities to embed reading, writing, communication and mathematics, as well as making links between new subject areas. This secondary collaboration will increase confidence and spread the Manglish message much faster between departments.

The overview for collaborative practice in this example is shown on the previous page.

What does success look like?

We have already seen how, during the planning process, teachers of maths and English will create shopping lists for the skills in their subjects and for the progression of these skills. To do the same, any teacher developing a Manglish approach should begin by asking what the end point is for a pupil at their school. The Manglish curriculum detailed here has been based on teaching English and maths in a typical school in England. The success criteria for differing levels of skill has been developed from looking at what is expected from a pupil achieving the top grades in English language and maths. This information can be found in the English and maths specifications for whatever course pupils are taking at Key Stage 4 (or the examination years at your school). You could simply copy the criteria presented to you in this book, but to get Manglish right in your school, you should really take into account your school's individual circumstances. A top-level pupil taking part in the example Manglish curriculum has the following skill set (see opposite:[2]

---

2 Adapted from the QCA/DCSF's National Strategies Mathematics Assessment Guidelines, Speaking and Listening Assessment Guidelines, Reading Assessment Guidelines and Writing Assessment Guidelines. These documents are no longer available from the Department for Education but a selection can be found at: <http://www.teachfind.com/>. All Manglish mats in the book are adapted from the same sources.

Writing	Communication	Using and applying mathematics
Sentence structures are used imaginatively and with precision to have specific effects throughout the text.	Pupils demonstrate that they can make creative selections from a wide repertoire of strategies and conventions to meet varied speaking and listening challenges.	Pupils confidently use their knowledge of mathematics to develop their own alternative methods and approaches to creating solutions.
Structural devices, language and techniques manipulate readers depending upon the purpose of the text.	Pupils consciously adapt their vocabulary, grammar and non-verbal features to any situation, including group-working roles, speeches, debates and drama.	Pupils select and combine known facts and problem-solving strategies to solve problems of increasing complexity.
Pupils have an original style and, thanks to a wide-ranging knowledge of text types and purposes, can manipulate different genres successfully. A range of viewpoints can be skilfully adopted with ease.	Pupils are able to sustain concentrated and sensitive listening; they respond with flexibility to creatively develop the ideas of others.	Pupils confidently convey mathematical meaning through the precise and consistent use of symbols.
Correct spelling and effective, imaginatively chosen, ambitious vocabulary is used throughout.	Pupils can exploit a range of dramatic approaches and techniques creatively to create complex and believable roles.	Pupils take nothing at face value and always further examine generalisations or solutions.
	Pupils have an excellent knowledge of spoken language features and continually reflect on their own and others' choices.	Pupils are able to comment constructively on the reasoning and logic of processes employed, with the ability to suggest alternative approaches which may produce more accurate results.

This is the starting point for the creation of your bespoke Manglish mats which will be developed and approved during your initial collaborative planning sessions. It is unlikely that a pupil arriving in your school at the start of Key Stage 3 will have these top-level skills already, nor will they all be working at the same level; therefore, teachers will need staged success criteria to support pupils' journeys towards this stage of operating. Teachers of English and maths will decide upon the levelled stages for success. This can be adapted from success criteria, such as examination materials or national curriculum level descriptors, or can be developed by the teachers themselves. If teachers develop their own criteria by examining the skills of their pupils at various stages of skill development, then they will own the criteria and, in turn, will be better able to put it into practice.

The criteria that you select will form the basis for your Manglish mats and will be used by all teachers in planning effective differentiated opportunities to build reading, writing, communication and maths into their subjects. Once teachers of English and maths have agreed on the staged levels of skills, they will work collaboratively with individual departments to adapt the criteria to suit that subject's content. (Examples of adapted Manglish mats and the lessons that were developed as a result of them appear in Chapter 2.) The mats are an important tool for supporting *all* teachers in delivering the Manglish curriculum – in their awareness of students' realistic abilities, what levels of reading, writing, communication and maths actually look like, and to help them recognise the opportunities that already exist in their subject areas that will support pupils in applying these skills in new and purposeful scenarios.

The subject-specific Manglish mats assist subject teachers when planning individual learning experiences during the year. For example, the example Manglish mat provided for half-term 1 (see pages 32–43) has been created for history teachers. Term-specific maths is included so that teachers are aware of the content of concurrent maths lessons. The reading, writing, communication and maths columns contain subject-specific suggestions based on the content of history lessons over that half-term. Teachers, like pupils, are individuals and should be given autonomy over the content of their lessons, as long as what they are delivering covers what the pupil needs to succeed in their subject, as well as providing opportunities to use the skills being taught in English and maths purposefully and effectively. The Manglish mat is a planning tool which enables teachers to avoid missed opportunities and supports them when creating challenge for their pupils' individual needs.

How you choose to label the levels in your Manglish mats is up to you. In the examples provided in this book, two separate mats have been created: an upper-ability red mat split into gold, silver and bronze sub-levels, and a lower-ability blue mat, again with gold, silver and bronze sub-levels. By organising mats in this way, you can encourage a school-wide system of three-way differentiation, giving pupils a consistent approach to how their individual needs are being catered for across the school. Examples of this system of differentiation can be found in the individual lessons detailed in Chapter 2. Teachers will collaborate to create differentiated resources that support pupils in progressing through the sub-levels towards success. Pupils should be made aware of their working-at levels and how the system is set up in your school – for example, a pupil working at **Blue Silver** will know that they need to aim for **Blue Gold** in order to improve.

How you label pupils' working-at levels is less important than teachers having a good understanding of what the label actually means. Teachers use the mats when planning their lessons by developing questions, activities and experiences that are tailored to create challenge at an appropriate level for their pupils. During planning, teachers will need to access pupils' realistic working-at levels. This data needs to be up to date and realistic, so that teachers across the school can plan the right level of challenge. English and maths teachers must regularly input data into a central spreadsheet which is accessible to teachers across the whole school. This is not data input for data input sake, which can be a painstaking and fruitless activity; this is data input for the sake of cross-curricular collaboration. It is worth it. With the right information, teachers can use the Manglish mat to assist them in the creation of tasks at the appropriate level. By splitting the levels into a series of colours, teachers can easily read the data and can use the correct criteria, specific to the pupils in their lessons, when developing their lessons.

Imagine a history teacher is about to plan a lesson in which the pupils will apply their writing skills to create a written report. The teacher accesses the pupils' data and sees that individual pupils differ in their current working-at levels for writing, but all pupils are within the blue mat – some being **Blue Gold,** some **Blue Silver** and some **Blue Bronze**. The teacher is able to provide each pupil with support materials appropriate to their working-at level because they have had support from English teaching colleagues during collaborative planning and can use the Manglish mat as a guide.

Teachers can also use the mats to identify opportunities that might ordinarily be missed. For example, during English lessons in half-term 2, pupils are developing their reading skills under the big idea of 'Big Brother'. Not *Big Brother* the TV series, but Big Brother in the Orwellian sense – the idea that we are under the microscope in our digital world. In science they are also examining human life as they look at humans as a species. Ordinarily, the science teacher would deliver only their own content; however, this science teacher has identified that his class are all working within the gold, silver and bronze levels of the blue mat and, using the reading column, recognises that pupils are applying the reading skills being taught in English while examining the source materials for their own subject. An opportunity to enhance the skills being taught in English has been identified and so the teacher uses the appropriate Manglish mat to construct realistic expectations of pupil responses based on their reading skills levels. This teacher knows that specific quotations should be encouraged as well as exploring the relia-bility of the source material in relation to its genre, audience and purpose.

No longer is a highly literate pupil being patronised, as the whole class is asked to spell the number 'one' for the nice Ofsted inspector's benefit; nor is a pupil with a high level of mathematical skill being asked to count the lines of a poem in English. Instead, teachers use Manglish mats to tailor expecta-tions and identify existing opportunities to apply English and maths skills in purposeful ways, no matter which subject they teach. The Manglish mats are a resource to be used by teachers but can be adapted to create success criteria for pupils too (see the GAP SPLITT planning section on pages 64–78). Chapters 2 and 3 provide examples of this in action.

As all teachers are collaborating and using the same criteria and knowledge of pupils' realistic working-at levels, pupils should begin to embed their skills and see what they are learning in maths and English as useful and transferable.

They will recognise how statistics can support their learning in geography and how being able to skim and scan can develop their knowledge acquisition in history. Pupils will soon recognise that all learning is inextricably linked. Great minds will emerge from a Manglish education – individuals who will see connections between all things. These great minds will shape our future.

You will find detailed lesson outlines and accompanying Manglish mats relating to history, citizenship, English and PE in Chapter 2. The table below is an example of a Manglish mat for history, which was developed using one school's criteria for reading, writing, communication and maths. History teachers would have collaborated with English and maths teachers to create this resource to support lesson planning, differentiation and progression.

Red Manglish Mat: History

	Reading	Writing
GOLD	Pupils have an ability to develop a clear critical stance on any text presented to them. They use texts to develop coherent interpretations of events.	Sentence structures are used imaginatively and with precision to have specific effects throughout the text.
	Pupils are able to make imaginative, insightful evaluations as a result of their wealth of knowledge of text types, purposes, audiences, language, structure and techniques.	Structural devices, language and techniques manipulate readers depending on the purpose of the text.
	Pupils' insights are always well supported by precise references and wider textual knowledge.	Pupils have an original style and, thanks to a wide-ranging knowledge of text types and purposes, can manipulate different genres successfully. A range of viewpoints can be skilfully adopted with ease.
	Pupils fully appreciate the overall effect of texts of various different genres over various time periods. They show clear understanding and critical evaluation of writers' purposes and viewpoints and how these are articulated throughout the text.	Correct spelling and effective, imaginatively chosen, ambitious vocabulary is used throughout.
	Pupils are independently critical of texts and their origins. They analyse and evaluate texts to determine for themselves how texts relate to particular contexts and traditions and how they may be received over time.	

Communication	Term-specific mathematics	Using and applying mathematics
Pupils demonstrate that they can make creative selections from a wide repertoire of strategies and conventions to meet varied speaking and listening challenges. Pupils consciously adapt their vocabulary, grammar and non-verbal features to any situation, including group-working roles, speeches, debates and drama. Pupils are able to sustain concentrated and sensitive listening; they respond with flexibility to creatively develop the ideas of others. Pupils can exploit a range of dramatic approaches and techniques creatively to create complex and believable roles. Pupils have an excellent knowledge of spoken language features and continually reflect on their own and others' choices.	Pupils can: Understand and use congruence and mathematical similarity. Understand and use trigonometrical relationships in right-angled triangles and use them to solve problems, including those involving bearings. Understand the difference between formulae for perimeter, area and volume in simple contexts by considering dimensions.	Pupils confidently use their knowledge of mathematics to develop their own alternative methods and approaches to creating solutions. Pupils select and combine known facts and problem-solving strategies to solve problems of increasing complexity. Pupils confidently convey mathematical meaning through precise and consistent use of symbols. Pupils take nothing at face value and always further examine generalisations or solutions. Pupils are able to comment constructively on the reasoning and logic of processes employed, with the ability to suggest alternative approaches which may produce more accurate results.

Red Manglish Mat: History

	Reading	Writing
SILVER	Pupils are developing an ability to choose their evidence precisely to support their arguments or conclusions. Pupils' ability to draw on knowledge of other sources to develop or clinch an argument is clearly developing as they have their own insights into texts after teasing out meanings and weighing up evidence. For example, they may reject an argument after exploring what is left unsaid and after comparing it to the rest of the evidence gathered. Pupils show an appreciation for a writer's use of language, structure and techniques and use their understanding of this to analyse texts for their purpose and effect. Pupils begin to independently analyse the context of a text, looking at its place in history and how it has been influenced by other texts to explore the viewpoint, purpose and effect on a range of audiences.	Pupils effectively use a variety of sentence types and punctuation to achieve purpose and overall effect. Pupils plan the organisation of the text with the purpose in mind. Paragraphs may flow effortlessly into each other or sections may stand out for increased clarity. Openings may be linked with endings to create the echo of an argument. Pupils create a range of texts with distinct and original viewpoints (not necessarily their own). When pupils are making vocabulary or technique choices, they think creatively about the effect on their purpose and audience. Pupils use correct spelling throughout and challenge themselves with their vocabulary choices.

Communication	Term-specific mathematics	Using and applying mathematics
Pupils are capable of using talk to explore a wide range of subjects. Planned talks are delivered to create specific effects upon different audiences. Pupils' choices of vocabulary, grammar and non-verbal features are apt and effective. Pupils can adapt easily to new audiences and purposes, including a variety of group-working roles. When listening to others, pupils are able to interrogate and extend upon what is said with well-judged questions delivered in a way that extends the speaker's thinking. When creating roles, pupils make insightful choices of speech, gesture, movement and dramatic approaches with confidence. Pupils' knowledge of spoken language allows them to evaluate the meaning and impact of how they and others use and adapt language for specific purposes.	Pupils can: Understand and apply Pythagoras' theorem when solving problems in 2D. Calculate lengths, areas and volumes in plane shapes and right prisms. Enlarge 2D shapes, given a centre of enlargement and a fractional scale factor (on paper and using ICT) and then recognise the similarity of the resulting shape. Find the locus of a point that moves according to a given rule, both by reasoning and using ICT. Recognise that measurements given to the nearest whole unit may be inaccurate by up to one half of the unit in either direction. Understand and use measures of speed, among other compound measures.	Pupils are able to use their mathematically reasoned research to evaluate future solutions. Pupils' confidence in the application of mathematics allows them to explore connections in mathematics across a range of contexts. Pupils appreciate the difference between a mathematical argument and experimental evidence. They are able to use and present both using a wealth of presentational structures. Pupils confidently justify their findings and create effective solutions based on accurately reasoned mathematical evidence.

Red Manglish Mat: History

	Reading	Writing
BRONZE	When using texts as evidence, pupils make relevant points, including summary and synthesis of information, from different sources or different places in the same text. Pupils' comments are securely based in textual evidence and they explore layers of meaning. Pupils recognise why the writer has structured the work in a specific way to create the overall effect on the reader. Pupils understand how the writer has used language and techniques and can trace them throughout a text to give a detailed explanation of the text as a whole. They begin to consider wider implications and layers of meaning when discussing this. Pupils use the context of a text to identify the writer's intended purpose and effect. They can easily identify the viewpoint of a text and its role in the purpose and effect. Pupils can discuss in detail how a text is affected by its context. Pupils recognise how the meaning and reception of a text can change over time and how conventions of text types can change over time.	Pupils use a full range of sentence structures and they are beginning to use them to manipulate their readers. Pupils are confident with their use of punctuation and use it to create effects. Before proofreading, pupils may still make errors with ambitious structures but can spot these errors before redrafting. When planning, pupils make choices about the structure of the text to have specific effects on the reader. Pupils plan to use certain language choices and techniques to create more convincing viewpoints. They are aware of the conventions associated with a range of text types and use this information to make their text convincing. Pupils use correct spelling throughout, including some ambitious, uncommon words. Pupils actively seek to increase their vocabulary.

Communication	Term-specific mathematics	Using and applying mathematics
Pupils can explore complex ideas in a range of ways. They are able to keep talk succinct or extended upon points for greater clarity. Pupils are controlled in their planned talks and guide listeners as a result of their structure. Pupils adapt vocabulary, grammar, and non-verbal features depending upon the situation.	Pupils can:	Pupils show confidence when identifying and solving mathematical problems.
Pupils can engage with complex discussion, adapting to any group role and listening to a range of points before making perceptive responses. They show an awareness of the speaker's aims and extended meanings but question them further, adding more to the discussion.	Classify quadrilaterals by their geometric properties.	Pupils recognise when it is sensible to order their investigations into smaller, more manageable tasks.
	Solve geometrical problems using properties of angles, of parallel and intersecting lines, and of triangles and other polygons.	When presenting their findings, pupils interpret, discuss and synthesise information in a variety of mathematical forms.
	Identify alternate and corresponding angles.	Their argument is effectively reasoned using symbols, diagrams, graphs and related explanatory texts, using logical argument to establish the truth of a statement.
	Understand that the sum of angles of a triangle is 180 degrees and of a quadrilateral is 360 degrees.	
Pupils are flexible in their choices of speech, gesture and movement, and can create different roles convincingly.	Devise instructions for a computer to generate and transform shapes and paths.	
	Visualise and use 2D representations of 3D shapes.	
Pupils have a wide-ranging knowledge of spoken language features and use them to recognise spoken language choices made by others.	Enlarge 2D shapes, given a centre of enlargement and a positive whole number scale factor.	
	Know that translations, rotations and reflections preserve length and angle, and map objects onto congruent images.	
	Use straight edges and compasses to do standard constructions.	
	Deduce and use formulae for the areas of a triangle and a parallelogram, and the volume of cuboids. They can also calculate volumes and surface areas of cuboids.	
	Know and use the formula for the circumference of a circle.	

Blue Manglish Mat: History

	Reading	Writing
GOLD	Pupils are selective about their use of evidence and can use quotations to back up their deductions about the text. Pupils infer meaning and deduce using examples from the text to back up their ideas. Pupils are able to identify how the text is organised and can refer to a range of features such as bullet points, paragraphs, headings and subheadings. Pupils are able to identify a range of language features used by the writer, with some explanation. Pupils can confidently identify text types for different purposes, such as leaflets, newspapers and articles. When identifying the main purpose of a text, pupils are able to comment on how the context of a text can affect the meaning. For example, they may recognise that facts found on Wikipedia may not be accurate.	Pupils use a full range of sentence structures for different purposes. Pupils can use a full range of punctuation correctly. They may make mistakes when attempting ambitious structures (e.g. 'Having studied the evidence, presented here as fact, it is clear that the numbers are incorrect, the numbers were found on Wikipedia.' Here the first use of commas for parenthesis is correct, but the second should be a semicolon as both sides of the comma could stand alone as sentences). Pupils plan their paragraphs to create a coherent and logical structure. Their openings and endings are effective. Connectives are used throughout to signal changes in time or message (e.g. therefore, however, unlike, before, meanwhile). Pupils plan their viewpoint and make vocabulary choices with the purpose and audience in mind. They are convincing. Pupils spell all common words correctly and no longer make mistakes with homophones. Pupils use dictionaries effectively to find new spellings. More complicated spellings may be incorrect (e.g. outrageous, exaggerated, announcing, parallel). Pupils should be provided with challenging topic-specific vocabulary lists.

Communication	Term-specific mathematics	Using and applying mathematics
Pupils elaborate on points to express and explain relevant ideas and feelings. Pupils plan what they say to make their meaning clear and to have an effect upon, as well as to engage, the listener.	Pupils can:	Pupils independently identify mathematical problems and are able to obtain the necessary information to come up with solutions.
	Use a wide range of properties of 2D and 3D shapes and identify all of the symmetries of 2D shapes.	
Pupils deliberately match vocabulary, grammar and non-verbal features to their audience, purpose and context.	Use language associated with angles and use the angle sum of a triangle and that of angles at a point.	Pupils apply their new learning from mathematics lessons to new investigations from a range of contexts.
When listening to others, pupils recognise implicit meanings and develop upon what has been said with comments and questions.	Reason about position and movement and transform shapes.	Pupils are confident when speaking using newly acquired mathematical language and interpreting symbols and diagrams to explain their own logical reasoning of problems.
Pupils are able to take on a range of roles in groups effectively and are able to take a leading role in shaping discussions, as well as developing characters beyond themselves through deliberate choices of speech, movement and gesture.	Measure and draw angles to the nearest degree, when constructing models and drawing or using shapes.	
	Read and interpret scales on a range of measuring instruments explaining what each labelled division represents.	
Pupils are able to explain features of their own and others' language use, showing understanding of the effect of varying language for different purposes and situations.	Solve problems involving the conversion of units and make sensible estimates of a range of measures in relation to everyday situations.	
	Understand and use the formula for the area of a rectangle and distinguish area from perimeter.	

Blue Manglish Mat: History

	Reading	Writing
SILVER	When using the text to support their ideas, pupils can refer to points in the text to back up their ideas but often paraphrase rather than make clear selections.	Pupils are beginning to use complex sentences, as well as simple and compound sentences, and they are learning to use subordinate clauses (e.g. 'After reviewing the findings, I found that men were less likely to make new friends when moving to a new country').
	When inferring meaning, pupils are able to refer to points in the text to explain why they think their ideas about it are correct.	Pupils write in the correct tense with occasional errors.
	Pupils are able to recognise why a text has been ordered in the way it has. For example, the writer uses bullet points.	Pupils can use full stops, capital letters, question marks, exclamation marks and speech marks without making mistakes. Pupils can use commas in lists and are learning to use them to indicate subordinate clauses.
	Pupils are able to pick out word classes and techniques, such as verbs or alliteration, and explain why the writer has chosen them.	Pupils plan topics for each of their paragraphs and begin each paragraph with a topic sentence. Ideas are in a logical order. Sentences are connected with more varied connectives, such as 'also' or 'then', but one or more can often be overused.
	Pupils can comment on the intended effect of a text on a reader.	Pupils can create a believable viewpoint and match it to their purpose and readers, although they are not always consistent.
	Pupils can recognise features common to different text types.	Pupils choose their vocabulary deliberately to match their purpose but are not overly ambitious with their choices.
	When identifying the main purpose of a text, pupils understand that writers have their own opinions and that it is important to know where a text is set and know who wrote it.	Pupils' spelling of common words is correct. This includes spelling rules for suffixes such as adding -ly and changing tense. Homophones may still be confused. Provide pupils with a unit-specific word bank to support spelling of new vocabulary.

Communication	Term-specific mathematics	Using and applying mathematics
Pupils are able to speak in extended turns to express their ideas and feelings. Pupils have given thought to how their listener may respond before they speak. As a listener, they consider what has been said and comment upon it, showing understanding. Pupils recognise that vocabulary, grammar and non-verbal features should be adapted, depending on their purpose and audience. Pupils understand the purpose of different roles in groups and show that they have attempted to adapt their talk to suit the needs of the situation. Pupils are able to create different roles and begin to make deliberate choices of speech, gesture, language and movement.	Pupils can: Use the properties of 2D and 3D shapes. Make 3D models by linking given faces or edges and draw common 2D shapes in different orientations on grids. Reflect simple shapes in a mirror line, translate shapes horizontally or vertically and begin to rotate a simple shape or object about its centre or a vertex. Choose and use appropriate units and instruments. Interpret, with appropriate accuracy, numbers on a range of measuring instruments. Find perimeters of simple shapes and find areas by counting squares.	Pupils are able to develop their own strategies for solving simple problems. They may choose to explore the effectiveness of war tactics using the number of deaths compared to the number of survivors, and present their findings using their choice of chart. Pupils can apply newly acquired mathematics to practical contexts. Pupils always present information and results in a clear and organised way.

Blue Manglish Mat: History

	Reading	Writing
BRONZE	Pupils can read a text fluently and use their understanding of phonetics to read unfamiliar words out loud. They can work out the meanings of new words.	Pupils' sentences are often basic. For example, using only simple sentences ('The mode means the most frequent') or compound sentences ('The mode is the most frequent and the median is the middle number').
	Pupils can recognise and retell the main points of the text.	Pupils will most commonly use 'and', 'but' and 'so' to connect sentences.
	Pupils can use the text as an example but will often retell the story of the text rather than using it to support their own ideas.	Pupils do not always use the right tense and may even switch between tenses without any purpose.
	Pupils can recognise word classes, such as adjectives, verbs, nouns and pronouns, within a text but do not comment on why they are used.	Pupils can use capital letters, full stops, exclamation marks and question marks in the right places.
	Pupils can recognise why a writer has written the text and can infer meaning.	Pupils will order their text logically but may not use clear paragraphs. They make links between ideas in the writing but some ideas may appear disjointed.
	Pupils can recognise differences and similarities between texts and the writers' viewpoints by inferring simple meanings.	Pupils can adopt a viewpoint. For example, if they are asked to write an example of pro-war propaganda, they will use positive vocabulary.
		Pupils may need support with setting out their work to match the style of the genre.
		Pupils use words that are appropriate to the set task but are not ambitious in their vocabulary choices.
		Common words are spelled correctly and unfamiliar words are often written phonetically. Pupils may need support with spelling and should be given unit-specific word banks. Homophones are likely to cause confusion (e.g. there, their, they're; too, two, to).

Communication	Term-specific mathematics	Using and applying mathematics
Pupils can present how they feel to one another by taking turns in extended speaking about a topic while maintaining eye contact and using gesticulation to further express their feelings.	Pupils can:	Pupils are able to select the mathematics they want to use, from a range provided by the teacher, to solve mathematical problems. They may choose to use a pie chart over a bar graph to better represent findings.
	Classify 2D and 3D shapes in various ways using mathematical properties such as reflective symmetry for 3D shapes.	
Pupils show that they are listening to other speakers' main ideas by making comments and suggestions.	Begin to recognise nets of familiar 3D shapes (e.g. cube, cuboid, square-based pyramid).	Pupils try out different simple mathematical approaches to find ways of overcoming problems.
Pupils try out different roles in groups and attempt to take on different viewpoints or roles by adapting what they say and how they say it.	Recognise shapes in different orientations and reflect shapes presented on a grid in a vertical or horizontal mirror line.	Pupils begin to organise their work logically and check their results are accurate. Pupils may use a calculator to check that survey results have been added up correctly.
	Describe position and movement.	
	Use a wider range of measures, including non-standard metric units and standard metric units of length, capacity and mass, in a range of contexts.	Pupils are able to use and interpret mathematical symbols and diagrams.
	Use standard units of time.	

2 Manglish in action

Thinking in Manglish

Manglish is a state of mind. To think in Manglish, you must break away from the confines of individual subjects and place your teaching as part of a whole education where links are made between all things. Great things can be achieved by subject specialists – they are experts in their line of work – but they should not compartmentalise themselves from the rest of the world. The greatest thinkers already think in Manglish and recognise that all things are intertwined.

For example, take an engineer commissioned to design an earthquake-resistant building. If this engineer were to think alone, she would almost certainly create a sound building. However, if the engineer were to look into the *history* of earthquake-resistant buildings, she would find examples of buildings that have stood the test of time. Structures that have survived countless earthquakes, such as the El Castillo pyramid at Chichen Itza, could provide her with knowledge about what already works and inspiration for a modern construction.[1] The engineer must also think about the *geography* of

---

1   El Castillo, in Mexico, has been standing since sometime between the ninth and twelfth centuries. The step-pyramid has withstood many earthquakes over the years and has been studied for its structural strength.

her building. What level of earthquake typically hits this region? What effects do earthquakes have on the land below the structure? What are the needs of the population? She must use *mathematics* to rationalise structural decisions, costing, probabilities … the list goes on. The engineer does not think of these subjects as separate – just that knowledge of all things is important in the process of creation. She is an engineering specialist but, as well as using her knowledge of other, let's say 'subjects', she recognises the role of all other subject specialists in making what they do successful.

When you are thinking in Manglish, you are not considering the examination at the end of this half-term. You are not thinking that you have to shoehorn in a writing task because you are supposed to be doing something Manglishy today. When you are thinking in Manglish, you have an excellent understanding of what reading, writing, communication and mathematical skills look like. You are aware of what is being taught across the curriculum at this time and you are able to spot opportunities that already exist within your subject to allow pupils to practise their newly acquired skills. You do not miss opportunities for enhancing pupils' skills; you collaborate effectively to create the best learning experiences possible for the pupils in your care.

If you have taken the plunge and followed all of the steps so far, you should now have a pretty solid plan of Manglish action. It is now time to get creative with your content. The following examples are just a taste of the possibilities that thinking in Manglish could create.

History, numbers and writing skills

The example history lesson that you will be guided through in this chapter comes from half-term 1 of the example year overview. The Manglish mat used to develop the criteria and support the teacher in recognising opportunities for reading, writing, communication and mathematics appears in full at the end of the lesson (on pages 52–63).

The content of the mathematics lessons in this half-term has been based on numbers, calculations and algebra, with a twist of magic. The maths teachers have set the scene for history by exploring the mathematics behind famous magicians who helped during the two world wars – such as Jasper Maskelyne, famous for his war-time illusions.[2] As a result of the cross-curricular collaboration, pupils are becoming increasingly aware that magic is not just card tricks and fluffy bunnies but is actually quite a complex science that has even been used to win wars – who knew? English lessons have focused on the writer as a magician and taught pupils to create magical stories using a GAP SPLITT planning structure. The details of this structure are explained on pages 64–78.

Meanwhile, during history lessons, pupils have been studying the Second World War in greater detail. They have been gaining knowledge of key events and learning the skills required to be a master historian, such as examining reliable sources and using evidence and facts effectively. In this lesson, pupils are about to apply their knowledge and skills from all three subjects in their end-of-unit Manglish project called 'Can the magic of misdirection save lives?'

Lesson outcome

What? To effectively use historical information to inform our tactical decisions.

How? Using mathematical reasoning to explore war-time tactics and creating a reasoned report.

Why? To know how historical events can support us in our present decision-making.

Connect

As pupils enter the room, the teacher places them in role as historians working for the prime minister. It is best if you get a colleague (perhaps one of the most serious looking and well-dressed members of the maths department!) to record a message as the prime minister. They should explain that as the world continues to decline into deep depression and more and more countries become bankrupt, the prime minister fears a repeat of the events in Germany during the Second World War when Hitler convinced a

---

2   Jasper Maskelyne (1902–1973) was a British magician who created many large-scale illusions during the Second World War.

desperate nation to go to war. Britain is now preparing for the worst. This invented scenario is not entirely realistic in our advanced world of satellites and digital communication, so you may want to explain to pupils that the 2008 financial crisis caused governments to shut down all satellite operations in order to save cash. However, it is a great way to get pupils thinking creatively about historical problems, examining reliable sources and creating sound solutions. After all, the reasoning behind the two world wars still being on the history curriculum is not (I hope) about planning for World War III!

As the country's best historians, pupils have been chosen to examine the events of the First and Second World Wars to explore the effectiveness of military operations. The Ministry of Defence are considering creating fake airfields to misdirect enemy fire. It is their job to report upon the effectiveness of this type of operation.

New information

Pupils are presented with the enquiry question: Can the magic of misdirection save lives? During the history lessons leading up to this point, pupils have been keeping detailed records of war-time events and have a range of information sources on which they can draw. Pupils have explored covert operations, such as the Starfish operation,[3] and have recorded key statistics such as:

> Number of attacks on farmland as a result of operation Starfish: 730
> Civilian lives lost during operation Starfish: 4
> Bombs dropped on average in one night: 100
> Lives lost during day one of Hitler's bombing campaign: 430
> Lives lost during the Blitz bombings: 60,000
> Number of sites: 230 airfields and 400 industrial sites
> Cost of fake Blenheims built for fake airfields: £400 (today's cost £18,500)
> Homes destroyed from bombing in Second World War: 2 million
> Cost of rebuilding one average two-bedroom home in 2013: £132,000

---

3   Starfish sites were used as decoys during the Blitz to simulate burning British cities and divert night-time bombing raids.

> Population of Britain post-Second World War: 47 million
> Civilian lives lost during Second World War: 62,000
> Population of Britain today: 62 million
> Number of active army soldiers today: 129,450
> Number of active soldiers needed throughout Second World War: 3.5 million[4]

Search for meaning

During the investigation, pupils must use and apply mathematical reasoning in order to form conclusions about the effectiveness of potential operations. This should be presented back to the prime minister as an informative report. Thanks to cross-curricular pupil planning guides (details to follow on pages 71–78) teachers are able to support pupils in their planning and creation of this report. The teacher has access to the central database of working-at levels for all pupils and can support them to make progress in writing at the level appropriate for them.

In the case of mathematics, this class contains pupils working at **Blue Gold**, **Blue Silver** and **Blue Bronze** levels. The teacher is able to use this information to determine what the pupils can and cannot do and to provide any support they may require in their mathematical reasoning. The teacher is prepared, through collaborative planning, to support pupils in the application of their mathematical knowledge during their investigation.

Blue Bronze: At this level, pupils still need support in applying mathematics to problems. They have been learning about using fractions in maths lessons and so should be supported in presenting historical numbers as fractions. Pupils are provided with examples of a range of simple methods to choose from to present their data, such as bar charts and pie charts, all of which they are familiar with from their maths lessons over this term. Pupils are given examples of how they might use historical statistics to work out the effectiveness of covert operations – for example, looking at the number of lives saved or lost as fractions of the population and making comparisons.

With the support of examples, pupils should be allowed to explore which methods are the most effective to illustrate these figures. For example,

---

4   These numbers are estimates based on Internet research.

pupils may use Excel to create the following simple bar chart. They realise that although it shows that far fewer civilians were killed as a result of operation Starfish, it is difficult to visualise the actual numbers and so they decide that it might be more effective to demonstrate the difference as fractions of the population.

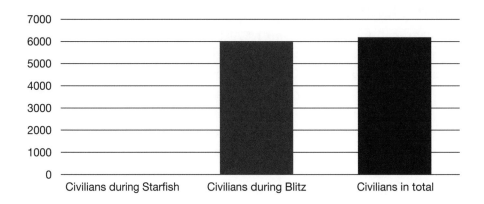

Blue Silver: The maths teachers of pupils working at a **Blue Silver** level have determined that these pupils are *more* independent when it comes to the choice of mathematics that they use to solve problems. Pupils may still need to see examples of how they might interpret the numbers, but this should be their choice. Pupils have been learning to understand fractions and ratios to solve problems and the teacher should encourage this link. Pupils are being provided with the opportunity to put mathematical reasoning into practice by exploring the available numbers from covert operations.

Blue Gold: Pupils at this level have been identified by their mathematics teachers as being able to create simple formulae; it may be possible for them to create their own formulae to represent the effectiveness of using covert operations during war. Pupils should be independent in their choice of what mathematics they use to present their findings to the prime minister. The teachers recognise that pupils have also been learning to reduce fractions to their simplest forms and so encourage this in their final presentation.

Demonstrate

Once pupils have completed their investigation, it is then written up as a formal report to be presented to the prime minister. Now pupils' writing skills come into play. The teacher has once again used the reading, writing, communication and mathematics database to determine what level of support pupils need with their writing skills. The class are all within the **Blue Silver** and the **Blue Gold** range. The teacher has once again used the Manglish mat during the planning of the task and effectively differentiates support resources by providing subject-specific word banks for the silver pupils, and for the gold pupils more challenging vocabulary as well as an expectation that they will discover their own new vocabulary.

The pupils use the cross-curricular GAP SPLITT planning structure that they have learned to use in English when writing up their report. The report is posted on a central blog so as to be accessible to all teachers. The pupils will receive personalised responses from the prime minister (aka their history teacher), directly via the blog.

Review

The history teacher is able to assess their pupils' historical accuracy and ability to perform a historical investigation. Maths and English teachers will also review the work for their written skill and application of mathematics. The English and maths teachers will not respond directly but will use the completed work to inform their own teaching. Pupils should perceive the joined-up approach to planning and feel that all outcomes are examined by all teachers. Putting their work on public display in this way gives writing an importance that writing up a report in a history exercise book may not.

The tables below are the red and blue Manglish mats that the history teachers used for planning and differentiation over this half-term.

Red Manglish Mat: History

Reading	Writing
Pupils have an ability to develop a clear critical stance on any text presented to them. They use texts to develop coherent interpretations of historical events.	Sentence structures are used imaginatively and with precision to have specific effects throughout the text.
Pupils are able to make imaginative, insightful evaluations as a result of their wealth of knowledge of text types, purposes, audiences, language, structure and techniques. Pupils' insights are always well supported by precise reference and wider textual knowledge.	Structural devices, language and techniques manipulate readers depending on the purpose of the text.
Pupils fully appreciate the overall effect of texts of various different genres and over various time periods. They show clear understanding and critical evaluation of writers' purposes and viewpoints and how these are articulated throughout the text.	Pupils have an original style and, thanks to a wide-ranging knowledge of text types and purposes, can manipulate different genres successfully. A range of viewpoints can be skilfully adopted with ease.
Pupils are independently critical of texts and their origins. They analyse and evaluate texts to determine for themselves how texts relate to particular contexts and traditions and how they may be received over time.	Correct spelling and effective, imaginatively chosen and ambitious vocabulary is used throughout.

Communication	Term-specific mathematics	Using and applying mathematics
Pupils demonstrate that they can make creative selections from a wide repertoire of strategies and conventions to meet varied speaking and listening challenges. Pupils consciously adapt their vocabulary, grammar and non-verbal features to any situation, including group-working roles, speeches, debates and drama. Pupils are able to sustain concentrated and sensitive listening; they respond with flexibility to creatively develop the ideas of others. Pupils can exploit a range of dramatic approaches and techniques creatively to create complex and believable roles. Pupils have an excellent knowledge of spoken language features and continually reflect on their own and others' choices.	Pupils can: Factorise quadratic expressions, including the difference of two squares (e.g. $x^2 - 9 = (x + 3)(x - 3)$). Understand the equivalence between recurring decimals and fractions. Use fractions or percentages to solve problems involving repeated proportional changes or the calculation of the original quantity given the result of a proportional change. Manipulate algebraic formulae, equations and expressions, finding common factors and multiplying two linear expressions. Solve problems involving calculating with powers, roots and numbers expressed in standard form, checking for correct order of magnitude and using a calculator as appropriate. Derive and use more complex formulae and change the subject of a formula. Evaluate algebraic formulae, substituting fractions, decimals and negative numbers. Solve inequalities in two variables and find the solution set. Sketch, interpret and identify graphs of linear, quadratic, cubic and reciprocal functions, and graphs that model real situations. Understand the effect on a graph of addition of (or multiplication by) a constant.	Pupils confidently use their knowledge of mathematics to develop their own alternative methods and approaches to creating solutions. Pupils select and combine known facts and problem-solving strategies to solve problems of increasing complexity. Pupils confidently convey mathematical meaning through the precise and consistent use of symbols. Pupils take nothing at face value and always further examine generalisations or solutions. Pupils are able to comment constructively on the reasoning and logic of processes employed, with the ability to suggest alternative approaches which may produce more accurate results.

Red Manglish Mat: History

	Reading	Writing
SILVER	Pupils are developing an ability to choose their evidence precisely to support their arguments or conclusions. Pupils' ability to draw on knowledge of other sources to develop or clinch an argument is clearly developing as they have their own insights on texts after teasing out meanings and weighing up evidence. For example, they may reject an argument after exploring what is left unsaid and after comparing it to the rest of the evidence gathered. Pupils show an appreciation for a writer's use of language, structure and techniques, and use their understanding of this to analyse texts for their purpose and effect. For example, they may discuss how the over-emotive language used in a political speech manipulates the listener's feelings on the subject. Pupils begin to independently analyse the context of a text, looking at its place in history and how it has been influenced by other texts to explore the viewpoint, purpose and effect on a range of audiences. For example, Second World War propaganda as influenced by that of the First World War.	Pupils effectively use a variety of sentence types and punctuation to achieve purpose and overall effect. Pupils plan the organisation of the text with the purpose in mind. Paragraphs may flow effortlessly into each other or sections may stand out for increased clarity. Openings may be linked with endings to create the echo of an argument. Pupils create a range of texts with distinct and original viewpoints (not necessarily their own). When pupils are making vocabulary or technique choices, they think creatively about the effect on their purpose and audience. Pupils use correct spelling throughout and challenge themselves with their vocabulary choices.

Communication	Term-specific mathematics	Using and applying mathematics
Pupils are capable of using talk to explore a wide range of subjects. Planned talks are delivered to create specific effects upon different audiences. Pupils' choices of vocabulary, grammar and non-verbal features are apt and effective. Pupils can adapt easily to new audiences and purposes, including a variety of group-working roles. When listening to others, pupils are able to interrogate and extend upon what is said with well-judged questions delivered in a way that extends the speaker's thinking. When creating roles, pupils make insightful choices of speech, gesture, movement and dramatic approaches with confidence. Pupils' knowledge of spoken language allows them to evaluate the meaning and impact of how they and others use and adapt language for specific purposes.	Pupils can: Square a linear expression, expand and simplify the product of two linear expressions of the form (x^n) and simplify the corresponding quadratic expression. Use algebraic and graphical methods to solve simultaneous linear equations in two variables. Solve inequalities in one variable and represent the solution set on a number line. Understand and use proportionality. Calculate the result of any proportional change using multiplicative methods. Understand the effects of multiplying and dividing by 0 and 1. Add, subtract, multiply and divide fractions, make and justify estimates and approximations of calculations. Estimate calculations by rounding numbers to one significant figure and use formulae from mathematics and other subjects. Substitute numbers into expressions and formulae, derive a formula and, in simple cases, change its subject by multiplying and dividing mentally. Find the next term and nth term of quadratic sequences and functions, explore their properties and plot graphs of simple quadratic and cubic functions (e.g. $y = x^2$, $y = 3 \times 2 + 4$, $y = x^3$). Use a calculator efficiently and appropriately to perform complex calculations with numbers of any size, knowing not to round during intermediate steps of a calculation.	Pupils are able to use their mathematically reasoned research to evaluate future solutions. For example, they may be able to state how, in a Third World War, nations could deploy their armies effectively so as to avoid the losses of the past. They would base their reasoning on mathematical evidence from the past. Pupils' confidence in the application of mathematics allows them to explore connections in mathematics across a range of contexts. Pupils appreciate the difference between a mathematical argument and experimental evidence. They are able to use and present both using a wealth of presentational structures. Pupils confidently justify their findings and create effective solutions based on accurately reasoned mathematical evidence.

Red Manglish Mat: History

	Reading	Writing
BRONZE	When using texts as evidence, pupils make relevant points, including summary and synthesis of information from different sources or different places in the same text. Pupils' comments are securely based in textual evidence and they explore layers of meaning. For example, when exploring connotations in a political speech or advertisement. Pupils recognise why the writer has structured the work in a specific way to create the overall effect on the reader. Pupils understand how the writer has used language and techniques and can trace them throughout a text to give a detailed explanation of the text as a whole. They begin to consider wider implications, layers of meaning and different audiences over different time periods when discussing this. Pupils use the context of a text to identify the writer's intended purpose and effect. They can easily identify the viewpoint of a text and its role in the purpose and effect. For example, the writer has chosen to look through the eyes of a wounded soldier to create sympathy in the audience. Pupils can discuss in detail how a text is affected by its context. Pupils recognise how the meaning and reception of a text can change over time and how conventions of text types can change over time.	Pupils use a full range of sentence structures and they are beginning to use them to manipulate their readers. Pupils are confident with their use of punctuation and use it to create effects. Before proofreading, pupils may still make errors with ambitious structures but can spot these errors before redrafting. When planning, pupils make choices about the structure of the text to have specific effects on the reader. For example, if they are creating a political speech, they may choose to emphasise a specific point at the start of each new topic (e.g. 'I have a dream'). Pupils plan to use certain language choices and techniques to create more convincing viewpoints. They are aware of the conventions associated with a range of text types and use this information to make their text convincing. Pupils use correct spelling throughout, including some ambitious, uncommon words. Pupils actively seek to increase their vocabulary.

Communication	Term-specific mathematics	Using and applying mathematics
Pupils can explore complex ideas in a range of ways. They are able to keep talk succinct or extend upon points for greater clarity. Pupils are controlled in their planned talks and guide listeners as a result of their structure. Pupils adapt vocabulary, grammar, and non-verbal features depending upon the situation. Pupils can engage with complex discussion, adapting to any group role and listening to a range of points before making perceptive responses. They show an awareness of the speaker's aims and extended meanings but question them further, adding more to the discussion. Pupils are flexible in their choices of speech, gesture and movement, and can create different roles convincingly. Pupils have a wide-ranging knowledge of spoken language features and use them to recognise spoken language choices made by others.	Pupils can: Use systematic trial and improvement methods and ICT tools to find approximate solutions to equations (e.g. $x^3 + x = 20$). Use the equivalence of fractions, decimals and percentages to compare/calculate percentages and find the outcome of a given percentage increase or decrease. Divide a quantity into two or more parts in a given ratio and solve problems involving ratio and direct proportion. Construct and solve linear equations with integer coefficients, using an appropriate method. Use proportional reasoning to solve a problem, choosing the correct numbers to take as 100% or as a whole. Generate terms of a sequence using term-to-term and position-to-term definitions of the sequence (on paper and using ICT) and write an expression to describe the nth term of an arithmetic sequence. Add and subtract fractions by writing them with a common denominator, calculate fractions of quantities (fraction answers), multiply and divide an integer by a fraction. Plot the graphs of linear functions, where y is given explicitly in terms of x, and recognise that equations of the form $y = mx + c$ correspond to straight-line graphs. Construct functions arising from real-life problems and plot their corresponding graphs, and interpret graphs arising from real situations.	Pupils show confidence when identifying and solving mathematical problems. Pupils recognise when it is sensible to order their investigations into smaller, more manageable tasks. For example, when investigating the overall effect of the First World War compared to the Second World War, pupils create spreadsheets to record specific statistics before converting them into percentages to compare. When presenting their findings, pupils interpret, discuss and synthesise information in a variety of mathematical forms. Their argument is effectively reasoned using symbols, diagrams, graphs and related explanatory texts, using logical argument to establish the truth of a statement. For example, if they were discovering which war had the greatest impact and where the impact was felt most, they may present death tolls, building costs, army costs, etc. as percentages proportionate to the country's starting point.

Blue Manglish Mat: History

	Reading	Writing
GOLD	Pupils are selective about their use of evidence and can use quotations to back up their deductions about the text. Pupils infer meaning and deduce using examples from the text to back up their ideas. Pupils are able to identify how the text is organised and can refer to a range of features (e.g. 'Each section starts with a question as if he's answering the crowd'). Pupils are able to identify a range of language features used by the writer with some explanation (e.g. 'When it gets to the climax they speak in short sentences and quickly which makes it more tense'). Pupils can easily identify the viewpoint of a text (e.g. 'The writer is strongly against war and wants to persuade the reader to agree'). Pupils can confidently identify text types for different purposes, such as leaflets, newspapers and diary entries. When identifying the main purpose of a text, pupils are able to comment on how the context of a text can affect the meaning. For example, a text written by a war survivor may be more biased than a historian's report of an event.	Pupils use a full range of sentence structures for different purposes. Pupils can use a full range of punctuation correctly. They may make mistakes when attempting ambitious structures (e.g. 'Rising from the ashes we, the people, will not be stopped, we shall succeed in our efforts against terrorism.' Here the first use of commas for parenthesis is correct, but the second should be a semicolon as both sides of the comma could stand alone as sentences). Pupils plan their paragraphs to create a coherent and logical structure. Their openings and endings are effective. Connectives are used throughout to signal changes in time or message (e.g. therefore, however, unlike, before, meanwhile). Pupils plan their viewpoint and make vocabulary choices with the purpose and audience in mind. They are convincing. Pupils spell all common words correctly and no longer make mistakes with homophones. Pupils use dictionaries effectively to find new spellings. More complicated spellings may be incorrect (e.g. outrageous, exaggerated, announcing, parallel). Pupils should be provided with challenging topic-specific vocabulary lists.

Communication	Term-specific mathematics	Using and applying mathematics
Pupils elaborate upon points to express and explain relevant ideas and feelings. Pupils plan what they say to make their meaning clear and to have an effect upon, as well as to engage, the listener. Pupils deliberately match vocabulary, grammar and non-verbal features to their audience, purpose and context. When listening to others, pupils recognise implicit meanings and develop upon what has been said with comments and questions. Pupils are able to take on a range of roles in groups effectively and are able to take a leading role in shaping discussions, as well as developing characters beyond themselves through deliberate choices of speech, movement and gesture. Pupils are able to explain features of their own and others' language use, showing understanding of effect of varying language for different purposes and situations.	Pupils can: Construct and express in symbolic form, and use simple formulae involving one or two operations. Use their understanding of place value to multiply and divide whole numbers and use known facts, place value, knowledge of operations and brackets to calculate and explain the effect. Use a calculator where appropriate to calculate fractions and percentages of quantities and measurements. Round decimals to the nearest decimal place and order negative numbers. Understand and use an appropriate non-calculator method for solving problems that involve multiplying and dividing any three-digit number by any two-digit number. Recognise and use number patterns and relationships to solve simple problems involving ordering, adding and subtracting negative numbers. Use equivalence between fractions and are able to order fractions and decimals. Reduce a fraction to its simplest form by cancelling common factors. Solve simple problems involving ratio and direct proportion.	Pupils independently identify mathematical problems and are able to obtain the necessary information to come up with solutions. For example, pupils recognise that by applying rules of ratio to the numbers they have collected from different countries of different sizes, the outcomes of the problem will be different. Pupils independently check results, considering whether these are reasonable. Pupils apply their new learning from mathematics lessons to new investigations from a range of contexts. Pupils are confident when speaking using newly acquired mathematical language and interpreting symbols and diagrams to explain their own logical reasoning of problems.

Blue Manglish Mat: History

	Reading	Writing
SILVER	When using the text to support their ideas, pupils can refer to points in the text to back up their ideas but often paraphrase rather than make clear selections. When inferring meaning, pupils are able to refer to points in the text to explain why they think their ideas about it are correct. Pupils are able to recognise why a text has been ordered in the way it has. For example, the writer uses bullet points to highlight their main points or describes the soldier's experience first to set the scene. Pupils are able to pick out word classes and techniques, such as verbs or alliteration, and explain why the writer has chosen them. For example, they may say that a writer has chosen to use the adjectives 'muddy' and 'dirty' as they reveal to the reader the soldiers' filthy conditions. Pupils can comment on the intended effect of a text on a reader. For example, they may say that a newspaper report only describes negative events because the writer wants the reader to agree that war is bad. Pupils can recognise features common to different text types. For example, pupils will recognise the presentational features of a newspaper report and know that a diary entry is presented differently. When identifying the main purpose of a text, pupils understand that writers have their own opinions and that it is important to know where a text is set and who wrote it.	Pupils are beginning to use complex sentences, as well as simple and compound, and they are learning to use subordinate clauses (e.g. 'After his political speech, Hitler returned to his home'). Pupils write in the correct tense with occasional errors. Pupils can use full stops, capital letters, question marks, exclamation marks and speech marks without making mistakes. Pupils can use commas in lists and are learning to use them to indicate subordinate clauses. Pupils plan topics for each of their paragraphs and begin each paragraph with a topic sentence. Ideas are in a logical order. Sentences are connected with more varied connectives, such as 'also' or 'then', but one or more can often be overused. Pupils can create a believable viewpoint and match it to their purpose and readers, although they are not always consistent. They elaborate on ideas by using expanded noun and adverbial phrases (e.g. 'The evil, disgraceful war …', 'Slowly coming to an end, the old man's war was over'). Pupils choose their vocabulary deliberately to match their purpose but are not overly ambitious with their choices. Pupils' spelling of common words is correct. This includes spelling rules for suffixes, such as adding -ly, and changing tense. Homophones may still be confused. Provide pupils with a unit-specific word bank to support spelling of new vocabulary.

Communication	Term-specific mathematics	Using and applying mathematics
Pupils are able to speak in extended turns to express their ideas and feelings. Pupils have given thought to how their listener may respond before they speak. As a listener, they consider what has been said and comment upon it showing understanding. Pupils recognise that vocabulary, grammar and non-verbal features should be adapted, depending on their purpose and audience. Pupils understand the purpose of different roles in groups and show that they have attempted to adapt their speech to suit the needs of their situation. Pupils are able to create different roles and begin to make deliberate choices of speech, gesture, language and movement.	Pupils can: Use simple formulae expressed in words. Use and interpret coordinates. Recognise and describe number patterns. Use a range of mental methods of computation. Recognise and describe number relationships, including multiples and factors, and recall multiplication facts up to 10 × 10 and quickly derive corresponding division facts. Use efficient written methods of addition and subtraction and of short multiplication and division; they check the reasonableness of results with reference to the context or size of numbers. Use place value to multiply and divide whole numbers by 10 or 100. Multiply a simple decimal by a single digit. Recognise approximate proportions of a whole and use simple fractions to solve problems with or without a calculator. They also order decimals to three decimal places as they begin to understand simple ratios.	Pupils are able to develop their own strategies for solving simple problems. They may choose to explore the effectiveness of war tactics using the number of deaths compared to the number of survivors, and present their findings using their choice of chart. Pupils can apply newly acquired mathematics to practical contexts. For example, they have just learned to work out percentages in mathematics lessons and so see that they can turn survey findings into percentages. Pupils always present information and results in a clear and organised way.

Blue Manglish Mat: History

<table>
<tr><th></th><th>Reading</th><th>Writing</th></tr>
<tr>
<td>BRONZE</td>
<td>

Pupils can read a text fluently and use their understanding of phonetics to read unfamiliar words out loud. They can work out the meanings of new words.

Pupils can recognise and retell the main points of the text.

Pupils can use the text as an example but will often retell the story of the text rather than using it to support their own ideas.

Pupils can recognise word classes, such as adjectives, verbs, nouns and pronouns, within a text but do not comment on why they are used.

Pupils can recognise why a writer has written the text and can infer meaning. For example, in a newspaper report about the war, they state that the writer is anti-war because they only describe negative events.

Pupils can recognise differences and similarities between texts and their writers' viewpoints by inferring simple meanings. For example, they may recognise that one text has a pro-war message and another is anti-war.

</td>
<td>

Pupils' sentences are often basic – for example, simple sentences (e.g. 'The war was over') or compound sentences ('The war is over and the army came home').

Pupils will most commonly use 'and', 'but' and 'so' to connect sentences.

Pupils do not always use the right tense for their writing and may even switch between tenses without any purpose.

Pupils can use capital letters, full stops, exclamation marks and question marks in the right places.

Pupils will order their text logically but may not use clear paragraphs. Links are made between ideas within the writing but some ideas may appear disjointed.

Pupils can adopt a viewpoint. For example, if they are asked to write an example of pro-war propaganda, they will use positive vocabulary. They may expand on their nouns with simple adjectives (e.g. 'The horrible war').

Pupils may need support with setting out their work to match the style of the genre.

Pupils use words that are appropriate to the set task but are not ambitious in their vocabulary choices.

Common words are spelled correctly and unfamiliar words are often written phonetically. Pupils may need support with spelling and should be given unit-specific word banks. Homophones are likely to cause confusion (e.g. there, their, they're; too, two, to).

</td>
</tr>
</table>

Communication	Term-specific mathematics	Using and applying mathematics
Pupils can present how they feel to one another by taking turns in extended speaking about a topic, while maintaining eye contact and using gesticulation to further express their feelings.

Pupils show that they are listening to other speakers' main ideas by making comments and suggestions.

Pupils try out different roles in groups and attempt to take on different viewpoints or roles by adapting what they say and how they say it. | Pupils can:

Recognise a wider range of sequences and are beginning to understand the role of = (equals).

Understand place value in numbers to 1,000 and derive associated division facts from known multiplication facts.

Use place value to make approximations.

Add and subtract two-digit numbers mentally.

Recognise negative numbers in contexts such as temperature.

Add and subtract three-digit numbers using a written method.

Use simple fractions that are several parts of a whole and recognise when two simple fractions are equivalent.

Multiply and divide two-digit numbers by 2, 3, 4 or 5, as well as 10, with whole-number answers and remainders.

Use mental recall of addition and subtraction facts to 20 in solving problems involving larger numbers.

Solve whole number problems, including those involving multiplication or division that may give rise to remainders.

They are also beginning to use decimal notation in contexts such as money. | Pupils are able to select the mathematics they want to use, from a range provided by the teacher, to solve mathematical problems. They may choose to use a pie chart over a bar graph to better represent their historical findings.

Pupils try out different, simple mathematical approaches to find ways of overcoming problems.

Pupils begin to organise their work logically and check their results are accurate. Pupils may use a calculator to check that survey results have been added up correctly.

Pupils are able to use and interpret mathematical symbols and diagrams. For example, pupils may use graphs representing birth or death rates to compare world wars. |

The GAP SPLITT planning method

What's it for?

Pupils are routinely asked to complete written tasks in most subjects, but they are not always executed with the same level of planning and attention to detail as would be expected in an English lesson. Planning written tasks is absolutely essential if the end product is going to be of a high quality. Pupils often do not see the point in planning and, as a result, written work lacks clear structure. Pupils who are great writers but do not plan the structure and content of their writing often write too much and there is a lack of whole-text coherence. I teach pupils the importance of planning in my English lessons but, as I have witnessed by reviewing the work of my pupils in a variety of other subjects, the need to plan does not always follow them.

Pupils need support to make links between what they are learning in English and its practical application elsewhere. Teachers should highlight the fact that when pupils learn how to plan and write to inform in great depth in English, they must also apply this knowledge when creating informative documents in history and science. Providing pupils with simple, generic and easily accessible cross-curricular planning mats is one way to develop these links. The mat below can be used by both teachers and pupils as a planning tool during writing preparation.

The GAP SPLITT planning structure originated from a method of planning that I call the three-point plan. I originally developed this method using the acronym GAP LIST (genre, audience and purpose – language, information, style and tone). The new structure was devised by Joseph Swan Academy's assistant head teacher for teaching and learning, Jane Hutchison, and me during the reformation of our Key Stage 3 curriculum. We created SPLITT (structure, presentation, language, information, tone and techniques) following collaboration with the school's English teachers to get a consensus about what would work for everyone.

During the early stages of curriculum planning, we also audited all subjects to create a list of writing purposes that subject teachers were asking pupils to use during the completion of written tasks.

Writing to Inform

Genre What form of writing am I creating? Newspaper/letter?
Audience Who am I writing for? Young/old/specialist?
Purpose Writing to **inform**

Structure

- Use a clear topic sentence to start
- Make sure you use paragraphs
- Use simple and compound sentences to make your message clear

Presentational Features

- Use bold print, underlining or italics to emphasise key words
- Use subheadings to make topics clear
- Decide whether bullet points and images are appropriate

Language

- Use technical terms that relate to the subject matter
- Use impersonal language
- Nouns and verbs predominate

Information

- Make sure your content matches your genre
- Make sure your content matches your audience
- Make sure your content matches your purpose

Techniques

- Use facts and opinions to make information clear
- Use rhetorical questions to signpost the reader
- Use statistics to support your view

Tone and voice

- Use third-person narrative voice
- Use a formal voice
- Use present tense as a rule

Plan all writing using GAP SPLITT

Stage 1: Identify your genre, audience and purpose – they are at the heart of everything you do.

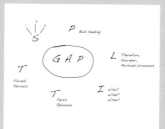

Stage 2: SPLITT up your planning. Use the guide and plan to match the needs of your genre, audience and purpose. Leave the S until last.

Stage 3: Plan your paragraph topics around the S using the information gathered in PLITT planning. Make links between your paragraphs.

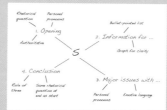

USE: .?,1'...();:"

This resulted in the following list:

> Persuasion
> Description
> Information
> Explanation
> Argument
> Analysis
> Review
> Evaluation

The English department agreed on a way of delivering the planning method to pupils and I used this information to create cross-curricular mats. A mat was created for every writing purpose delivered in school and this was placed into pupil and teacher planners for easy access during lessons.

Before the implementation of the planning mats, one geography teacher admitted that, during assessment of written work, they had only been looking at the content of the end product. This was found to be the case in many other areas of the curriculum. Pupils were clearly producing work with different levels of written skill but the teacher felt unable to comment on the quality of the writing, opting instead to look only at subject content. Whether through lack of confidence or a need to ensure delivery of their own subject content, pupils were creating written work with very little input on their written skill from the teacher. By comparing the descriptive work of one class completed in English to a similar descriptive task completed in geography, I found that, before using the mats, pupils did not apply the skills learned in English to the geography task. After implementing the mats, the teacher – aware that pupils had been taught to plan using the GAP SPLITT structure – asked pupils to use the mat and their previous learning in English. Pupils used the mats effectively, resulting in high quality written work that matched the standard produced in English.

Now add a Manglish mat to the mix (for clarification, I use the term Manglish mat solely for the planning tool used by teachers). Imagine that the teacher has planned a written task, complete with differentiated success criteria at an appropriate level of challenge for the pupils' realistic working-at levels. The teacher has collaborated with the English department during planning and, by using the Manglish mat as part of the process, has become confident in identifying levels of written skill. During the lesson, pupils create quality written work by using their learning from English, supported by planning mats, and the teacher is able to offer a realistic critique of pupils' written work in order to further improve their writing skills. The teacher is now self-assured in identifying different levels of writing and, most importantly, is confident in supporting pupils in making improvements. The teacher also has the tools, the confidence and the knowledge to use their own subject to support pupils' literacy skills.

The English teacher's role in GAP SPLITT

In order for the mats to be effective, all English teachers must teach pupils the same planning method when delivering writing skills (our school's guide is detailed below but you could develop your own). If a teacher from another subject asks pupils to take out their GAP SPLITT guide and the pupils have no idea what this means, the mats become useless. Teachers from other subjects should be aware of the planning method in order to support pupils in their application of skills, but they should not have to spend time delivering the method to pupils. Pupils should be *applying skills taught in English*, not *being taught English* by other subject teachers. The guide is there to support pupils in their application of skills; if teachers of other subjects are forced to teach writing skills as well as their own content, time is wasted and collaboration has failed to take place.

In our school, English teachers teach pupils how to plan using the GAP SPLITT guide in the following way:

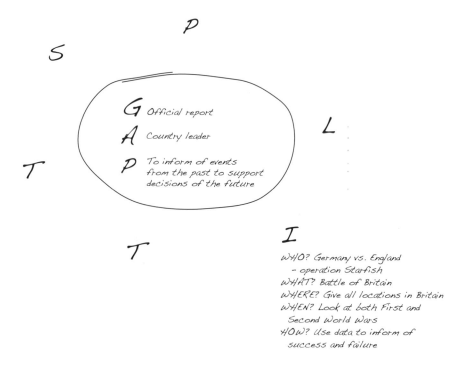

Stage 1: The pupil must identify the *genre* (newspaper, leaflet, website, etc.), *audience* (young, old, parents, lawyers, etc.) and *purpose* (inform, explain, describe) of their written task. GAP goes at the heart of their plan as it is key to getting all the other ingredients right. Ask pupils to write this information in the centre of a blank page – this will remind them of its importance. They will be referring back to it throughout their planning.

Stage 2: The pupil is taught to SPLITT up their planning, starting by writing the letters SPLITT around the outside of their plan. They should start with I (for *information*) and ask themselves: Who? What? Where? When? Why? to begin forming a list of the correct information required in their writing to match their GAP.

Pupils can then fill in the rest of the SPLITT plan in the order of their choice, but they should leave the S until Stage 3. The first T stands for the *tone* of the writing – pupils will use the mat to support them in finding the appropriate voice for their work. For example, in the task set in history, pupils use the Writing to Inform mat to remind themselves that their writing should be written in 'third-person narrative' and 'use a formal voice'. *Techniques* come next. When writing in other subjects, pupils can use their mat to remind them of the techniques that are most commonly found in the specific writing type they are being asked to create. Their English teacher will have taught pupils to recognise and use a much more extensive range of techniques than are presented on the mat. However, the mat must be kept simple so that it is accessible for all. Next, pupils decide what *presentational* devices are effective for their work, and end Stage 2 by creating a vocabulary list, appropriate to their GAP, as they make choices about their use of *language*. At the end of Stage 2, the plan will look something like this:

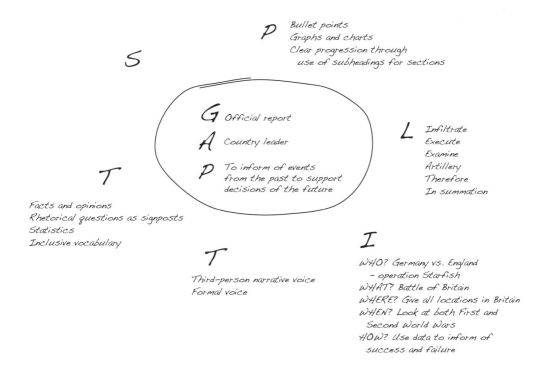

Stage 3: The *structure* of the writing is the final stage, as pupils must know what the writing will contain before they can create an effective structure. Pupils should plan paragraphs or sections around the structure. Pupils who are working at a **Blue Gold** level or higher for writing will also be taught how to link paragraphs or sections together by looking at their last and first sentences, as well as the content of their paragraphs to create a more cohesive text. Pupils at all levels should be separating their writing into clear paragraphs. Within each paragraph is a focus topic and pupils should identify the main topic of each paragraph during this stage of planning. The completed S section will look something like this:

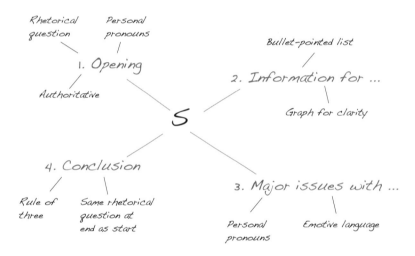

Planning should typically take pupils around ten to fifteen minutes. The plan they create will be very simple but gives pupils time to organise the content of their writing around the genre, audience and purpose of any writing task. The English teacher's role is to support pupils in becoming comfortable with planning for a range of writing purposes. Teachers of all other subjects must also support pupils in the application of these skills by asking them to use the planning mats when creating written tasks in their subjects.

Here are some example planning mats for our eight identified writing purposes: describe, inform, persuade, explain, argue, analyse, evaluate and review.

Writing to Describe

Genre What form of writing am I creating? Newspaper/letter?
Audience Who am I writing for? Young/old/specialist?
Purpose Writing to **describe**

Structure

- Start with a sequence of long, descriptive sentences followed by a short dramatic sentence
- Make sure you use paragraphs
- Vary your sentences to include simple, compound and complex

Presentational Features

- Use bold print, underlining or italics to emphasise key words
- Use a title that emphasises the content
- Bullet points and subheadings are *not* appropriate

Language

- Use adjectives and adverbs to develop description
- Use emotive/dramatic language to engage, thinking carefully about your word choice
- Use discourse markers to lead the reader through your writing

Information

- Make sure your content matches your genre
- Make sure your content matches your audience
- Make sure your content matches your purpose

Techniques

- Use metaphors or similes to create clear images for your reader
- Use alliteration or onomatopoeia to develop sound imagery
- Use personification as a way of bringing objects to life

Tone and voice

- Decide whether to use first-person or third-person narrative voice
- Decide upon a mood and use words that reflect it
- Decide whether to use past or present tense

Plan all writing using GAP SPLITT

Stage 1: Identify your genre, audience and purpose – they are at the heart of everything you do.

Stage 2: SPLITT up your planning. Use the guide and plan to match the needs of your genre, audience and purpose. Leave the S until last.

Stage 3: Plan your paragraph topics around the S using the information gathered in PLITT planning. Make links between your paragraphs.

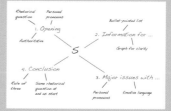

USE: .?,1'...();:"

Writing to Inform

Genre What form of writing am I creating? Newspaper/letter?
Audience Who am I writing for? Young/old/specialist?
Purpose Writing to **inform**

Structure

- Use a clear topic sentence to start
- Make sure you use paragraphs
- Use simple and compound sentences to make your message clear

Presentational Features

- Use bold print, underlining or italics to emphasise key words
- Use subheadings to make topics clear
- Decide whether bullet points and images are appropriate

Language

- Use technical terms that relate to the subject matter
- Use impersonal language
- Nouns and verbs predominate

Information

- Make sure your content matches your genre
- Make sure your content matches your audience
- Make sure your content matches your purpose

Techniques

- Use facts and opinions to make information clear
- Use rhetorical questions to signpost the reader
- Use statistics to support your view

Tone and voice

- Use third-person narrative voice
- Use a formal voice
- Use present tense as a rule

Plan all writing using GAP SPLITT

Stage 1: Identify your genre, audience and purpose – they are at the heart of everything you do.

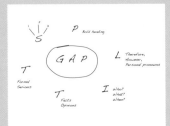

Stage 2: SPLITT up your planning. Use the guide and plan to match the needs of your genre, audience and purpose. Leave the S until last.

Stage 3: Plan your paragraph topics around the S using the information gathered in PLITT planning. Make links between your paragraphs.

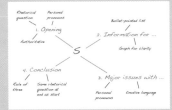

USE: .?,1'...();:"

Writing to Persuade

Genre What form of writing am I creating? Newspaper/letter?
Audience Who am I writing for? Young/old/specialist?
Purpose Writing to **persuade**

Structure

- Use a short, dramatic opening sentence, which may include imperatives
- Make sure you use topic-specific paragraphs
- Include simple, compound and complex sentences

Presentational features

- Use bold print, underlining or italics to emphasise key words
- Include illustrations that are clearly linked to the content
- Decide whether bullet points and subheadings are appropriate

Language

- Use personal pronouns such as 'you' to involve the reader
- Use emotive/dramatic language to engage, thinking carefully about your word choice
- Use discourse markers to develop your persuasion

Information

- Make sure your content matches your genre
- Make sure your content matches your audience
- Make sure your content matches your purpose

Techniques

- Use rhetorical questions to make the reader question themselves
- Use repetition to emphasise a point
- Use facts and opinions to support your point of view

Tone and voice

- Decide whether to use first-person or third-person narrative voice
- Decide whether this is an informal or formal piece
- Decide whether to use past or present tense

Plan all writing using GAP SPLITT

Stage 1: Identify your genre, audience and purpose – they are at the heart of everything you do.

Stage 2: SPLITT up your planning. Use the guide and plan to match the needs of your genre, audience and purpose. Leave the S until last.

Stage 3: Plan your paragraph topics around the S using the information gathered in PLITT planning. Make links between your paragraphs.

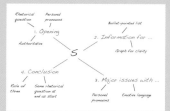

USE: .?,1'...();:"

Writing to Explain

Genre What form of writing am I creating? Newspaper/letter?
Audience Who am I writing for? Young/old/specialist?
Purpose Writing to **explain**

Structure

- Start with a clear topic sentence which answers the questions 'how?' or 'why?' End with a summary statement
- Make sure you use paragraphs which outline clear steps
- Use simple and compound sentences to make your message clear

Presentational features

- Use bold print, underlining or italics to emphasise key words
- Use subheadings to make topics clear
- Decide whether bullet points and images are appropriate

Language

- Use technical terms that relate to the subject matter
- Use impersonal language
- Use a minimum of adjectives and adverbs; instead include nouns and verbs

Information

- Make sure your content matches your genre
- Make sure your content matches your audience
- Make sure your content matches your purpose

Techniques

- Use facts and opinions to make information clear
- Use anecdotes to highlight the explanation
- Use statistics to support your view

Tone and voice

- Use third-person narrative voice
- Use a formal voice
- Use present tense as a rule

Plan all writing using GAP SPLITT

Stage 1: Identify your genre, audience and purpose – they are at the heart of everything you do.

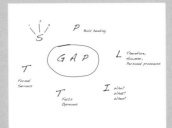

Stage 2: SPLITT up your planning. Use the guide and plan to match the needs of your genre, audience and purpose. Leave the S until last.

Stage 3: Plan your paragraph topics around the S using the information gathered in PLITT planning. Make links between your paragraphs.

USE: .?,1'...();:"

Writing to Argue

Genre What form of writing am I creating? Newspaper/letter?
Audience Who am I writing for? Young/old/specialist?
Purpose Writing to **argue**

Structure

- Open your argument with a sentence that clearly states your point of view
- Use paragraphs with clear topics to support your argument
- Use simple, compound and complex sentences

Presentational features

- Use bold print, underlining or italics to emphasise key words
- Use a title that emphasises the content
- Bullet points and subheadings may *not* be appropriate

Language

- Use personal pronouns such as 'you' to involve the reader
- Use emotive/dramatic language to engage, thinking carefully about your word choice
- Use discourse markers to develop your argument

Information

- Make sure your content matches your genre
- Make sure your content matches your audience
- Make sure your content matches your purpose

Techniques

- Use the rule of three to develop your ideas
- Use hyperbole to exaggerate your opinions
- Use anecdote to demonstrate your points to your reader

Tone and voice

- Be direct and to the point
- Use politeness and tact to help win over your reader
- Make sure you sound knowledgeable about your side of the argument and in your consideration of the counter-argument

Plan all writing using GAP SPLITT

Stage 1: Identify your genre, audience and purpose – they are at the heart of everything you do.

Stage 2: SPLITT up your planning. Use the guide and plan to match the needs of your genre, audience and purpose. Leave the S until last.

Stage 3: Plan your paragraph topics around the S using the information gathered in PLITT planning. Make links between your paragraphs.

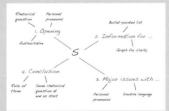

USE: .?,1'...():"

Writing to Analyse

Genre What form of writing am I creating? Newspaper/letter?
Audience Who am I writing for? Young/old/specialist?
Purpose Writing to **analyse**

Structure

- Open and close your work with a clear introduction and conclusion
- Use simple, compound and complex sentences
- Use PEA (point–evidence–analysis) as a structure for your paragraphs

Presentational features

- Use bold print, underlining or italics when naming a book, programme or film
- Use a title that emphasises the content
- Bullet points and subheadings are *not* appropriate

Language

- Use a writer's/creator's second name when referring to them throughout the essay
- Use appropriate adjectives to describe characters, etc.
- Use discourse markers to lead your reader through your ideas

Information

- Make sure your content matches your genre
- Make sure your content matches your audience
- Make sure your content matches your purpose

Techniques

- Use anecdotes to help further analyse points
- Create parallel structures that help compare points
- Use rhetorical questions to begin analysis of a new point

Tone and voice

- Write in a lively fashion showing a passion for your topic
- Use an authoritative tone and avoid 'I think … I feel …'
- Show careful consideration of the topic on a personal level

Plan all writing using GAP SPLITT

Stage 1: Identify your genre, audience and purpose – they are at the heart of everything you do.

Stage 2: SPLITT up your planning. Use the guide and plan to match the needs of your genre, audience and purpose. Leave the S until last.

Stage 3: Plan your paragraph topics around the S using the information gathered in PLITT planning. Make links between your paragraphs.

USE: .?,1'…();:"

Writing to Evaluate

Genre What form of writing am I creating? Newspaper/letter?
Audience Who am I writing for? Young/old/specialist?
Purpose Writing to **evaluate**

Structure

- Start with a clear topic sentence to which answers the questions 'how?' or 'why?' End with a summary
- Make sure you use paragraphs which outline clear steps
- Use simple and compound sentences throughout

Presentational features

- Use bold print, underlining or italics to emphasise key words
- Use subheadings to make topics clear
- Decide whether bullet points and images are appropriate

Language

- Use technical terms that relate to the subject matter
- Use minimal imagery, instead keeping ideas clear
- Use appropriate nouns, verbs and adjectives to help describe your process

Information

- Make sure your content matches your genre
- Make sure your content matches your audience
- Make sure your content matches your purpose

Techniques

- Use facts and opinions to make information clear
- Use anecdotes from the process to highlight the explanation
- Use statistics gained throughout the process to support your evaluation

Tone and voice

- Sound like an expert in the topic you are evaluating
- Use an authoritative tone
- Look back on your process using the past tense but allude to the future using your reflections as a guide

Plan all writing using GAP SPLITT

Stage 1: Identify your genre, audience and purpose – they are at the heart of everything you do.

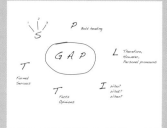

Stage 2: SPLITT up your planning. Use the guide and plan to match the needs of your genre, audience and purpose. Leave the S until last.

Stage 3: Plan your paragraph topics around the S using the information gathered in PLITT planning. Make links between your paragraphs.

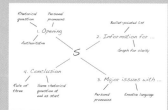

USE: .?,1'...0;:"

Writing to Review

Genre What form of writing am I creating? Newspaper/letter?
Audience Who am I writing for? Young/old/specialist?
Purpose Writing to **review**

Structure

- Capture your reader with a sentence that clearly states your point of view about what you are reviewing
- Remember to use paragraphs
- Use simple, compound and complex sentences

Presentational features

- Use bold print, underlining or italics to emphasise key words
- Use subheadings to make topics clear
- Decide whether bullet points and images are appropriate

Language

- Use a writer's/creator's second name when referring to them throughout the review
- Use appropriate and lively adjectives to describe characters etc.
- Use discourse markers to lead your reader through your ideas

Information

- Make sure your content matches your genre
- Make sure your content matches your audience
- Make sure your content matches your purpose

Techniques

- Use a pun to add humour to your review
- Use alliteration to create sound imagery
- Use similes to create images to help your reader imagine the topic you are reviewing

Tone and voice

- Write in a lively fashion, showing a passion for your topic
- Use colloquial language to engage your reader
- Show a careful, well-considered appreciation of the topic

Plan all writing using GAP SPLITT

Stage 1: Identify your genre, audience and purpose – they are at the heart of everything you do.

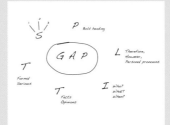

Stage 2: SPLITT up your planning. Use the guide and plan to match the needs of your genre, audience and purpose. Leave the S until last.

Stage 3: Plan your paragraph topics around the S using the information gathered in PLITT planning. Make links between your paragraphs.

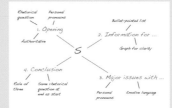

USE: .?,1'...();:"

Citizenship and reading skills

During half-term 2, pupils have been learning to read for meaning in English and have also been exploring the idea of Big Brother, in the Orwellian sense. The Manglish mat that was developed by the teachers involved in the creation of this session can be found at the end of this lesson (pages 84–95). Pupils are learning to correctly reference texts and use them to support their arguments. In this lesson, the class has been identified as being **Red Gold**, **Red Silver** and **Red Bronze** when it comes to reading for meaning, so the citizenship teacher knows that a high level of challenge and expectation should be employed when exploring texts that support their learning in this subject.

Following the big idea for the term, the teacher is focusing on the precious liberties enjoyed by citizens of the UK and their right to privacy. There are between 4 and 5 million CCTV cameras in operation throughout Britain today; this is a controversial subject with many citizens feeling that surveillance cameras represent an invasion of privacy. Should your every move be watched? The pupils of this class are about to undertake an investigation into this very topic.

Lesson outcome

What? To exercise an opinion based upon fact.

How? By exploring the literature behind CCTV to make critical judgements about its effectiveness and necessity.

Why? As British citizens, we have a right to voice our opinions. Privacy is a very important issue, so we should be fully informed before articulating our views.

Connect

The classroom has been set up so that pupils are working in groups of four. The teacher has previously determined the working groups and arranged tables according to reading ability to support the easy distribution of differentiated materials. Facing each desk is a recording device which is switched to record – every move the pupils make is being watched. The intended effect upon the pupils is that they should feel uncomfortable as they are being recorded from the moment that they enter the room. Groups are provided with one A1 sheet of paper and each pupil has a red pen. Pupils are asked to write down adjectives to describe the way the situation makes them feel – they are given a few moments to discuss this first. Their list might look something like this: uncomfortable, unnerved, watched, creeped out, nervous, on edge, exposed, etc. The writing is in red as pupils will change the colour of their pens throughout the lesson to demonstrate the progression of their thoughts.

The teacher asks pupils to share their thoughts and the class decide that being watched creates negative emotions within them. The teacher then asks them if they are doing anything that they should be ashamed of. The class, barring little Jimmy who quietly removes the chewing gum from his mouth, reply that they are not.

New information

The teacher uses the idea that being watched causes negative emotions to introduce the debate on CCTV. The enquiry question 'Should Big Brother be watching us?' is posed. Pupils are asked to investigate the question in teams and read more about the topic to develop a bank of evidence to support their arguments. To support them in developing their reading skills, the teacher provides each group with guidance on how they might approach the task. The teacher has been collaboratively planning with the English department over this half-term and has produced support materials under their guidance to enable pupils to apply reading skills from English in this new context. Pupils are also provided with reading source materials, such as newspaper stories, online articles and blogs to get them started.

Red Bronze: Pupils are provided with detailed prompt questions and material to support them in their exploration. Pupils at this level are confident in their ability to analyse but may need support in being reminded of the process.

> Use the support materials to find evidence to argue for or against Big Brother watching us every day. You should highlight key quotations that support your argument for later use.

After reading the support materials, consider the following: Who wrote the text? Where and when? What effect does this have on its reliability? Who is the intended audience and what is the text's intended purpose? Does this affect the text's reliability?

After determining the reliability of your texts, review your quotations for their use of language.

Quotations that are based in fact are more likely to create a stronger argument than overly emotional or non-committal quotations.

Red Silver: Pupils at this level are becoming more independent in their analysis of texts. Pupils are provided with the following prompts:

Use the support materials to find evidence to argue for or against Big Brother watching us every day.

Consider the following before choosing a quotation: the genre, audience and purpose of the text, the text's origins and the language, information and tone.

Red Gold: Pupils at this level are highly capable of developing critical responses but still need guidance to remind them to link their learning in English to this reading task. Pupils should be challenged in their abilities and the teacher's expectations are high.

Use the support materials and your wider reading to develop a clear critical stance on whether Big Brother should be watching us every day.

When considering the effectiveness of text choices in supporting your argument, remember to consider genre, audience, purpose, language, information, style and tone.

As well as the examples provided by the teacher, pupils should all have access to wider reading materials, if possible, to allow them to read widely on the topic – smartphones, tablets or computers are perfect to enable them to locate online articles.

Search for meaning

Pupils should change their pen colour after reading each article and, as their feelings and understanding about CCTV develop, they should continue to add to their A1 sheet. As pupils read documents that demonstrate the positive effects of CCTV (e.g. the Human Rights Act, the twelve-point code of practice for surveillance cameras), their lists may begin to appear less negative, and begin to contain words such as: safe, secure, crime free, protected. However, pupils may also read negative reports about the misuse of CCTV, which may draw their vocabulary back to the negative: mistrust, misused, misinterpreted. This vocabulary bank will support them in preparation for their later debate.

Demonstrate

Pupils are provided with slips of paper and should record on them their chosen quotations, along with correct citations stating the source. A space on the classroom wall has been cleared to place the quotations. The teacher then leads a debate on whether CCTV should or should not be allowed on the streets of Britain. Pupils use their vocabulary banks to describe an honest journey through their learning today as they join in the discussion. An excellent response, which shows that the pupil has engaged with the reading material to create an informed critical stance, might sound like this:

> Upon entering the room today, the use of CCTV unnerved me. I felt exposed, although I had done nothing wrong. This feeling was further enhanced as I first read the story of Mr Robson, the man accused of antisocial behaviour as he 'resembled the images of a man caught on CCTV'. Had I remained at this point, I would have continued to feel uncertain and suspicious of the role of CCTV as its images in this case were misinterpreted. However, I felt that this was an overly emotional story written for a tabloid newspaper. Mr Robson was 'never convicted' and the case was 'thrown out of court'. The use of hyperbolic statement throughout the report led me to mistrust

its integrity as quality evidence and so I went on to read the Protection of Freedoms Act 2012. Being a factual government document, this felt a more trustworthy source. After reading that 'the disclosure of images and information should only take place when it is necessary for such a purpose or for law enforcement purposes', I began to feel safe and secure knowing that Big Brother is not watching me to know my every move. Big Brother is watching 'to support safety and law enforcement'. And I believe that Big Brother should continue to watch us all.

Review

Pupils in this lesson have been given the opportunity to practise their ability to extract evidence for a real purpose. As a citizen of Britain, they are allowed to express their views but they should be making informed choices when doing so. This is a high-achieving class, so they are challenged not only to explore the facts but to determine the reliability of the sources – thereby supporting their reading skills for life.

The following tables are the red and blue Manglish mats used by citizenship teachers to plan and differentiate over this half-term.

Red Manglish Mat: Citizenship

	Reading	Writing
GOLD	Pupils have the ability to develop a clear critical stance on any text presented to them. They use texts to develop coherent interpretations of historical events.	Sentence structures are used imaginatively and with precision to have specific effects throughout the text.
	Pupils are able to make imaginative, insightful evaluations as a result of their wealth of knowledge of text types, purposes, audiences, language, structure and techniques. Pupils' insights are always well supported by precise references and wider textual knowledge.	Structural devices, language and techniques manipulate readers depending upon the purpose of the text.
	Pupils fully appreciate the overall effect of texts of various different genres over various time periods. They show clear understanding and critical evaluation of writers' purposes and viewpoints and how these are articulated throughout the text.	Pupils have an original style and, thanks to a wide-ranging knowledge of text types and purposes, can manipulate different genres successfully. A range of viewpoints can be skilfully adopted with ease.
	Pupils are independently critical of texts and their origins. They analyse and evaluate texts to determine for themselves how texts relate to particular contexts and traditions and how they may be received over time.	Correct spelling and effective, imaginatively chosen, ambitious vocabulary is used throughout.

Communication	Term-specific mathematics	Using and applying mathematics
Pupils demonstrate that they can make creative selections from a wide repertoire of strategies and conventions to meet varied speaking and listening challenges. Pupils consciously adapt their vocabulary, grammar and non-verbal features to any situation, including group-working roles, speeches, debates and drama. Pupils are able to sustain concentrated and sensitive listening, and they respond with flexibility to creatively develop the ideas of others. Pupils can exploit a range of dramatic approaches and techniques creatively to create complex and believable roles. Pupils have an excellent knowledge of spoken language features and continually reflect on their own and others' choices.	Pupils can: Estimate and find the median, quartiles and interquartile range for large data sets, including using a cumulative frequency diagram. Compare two or more distributions and make inferences, using the shape of the distributions and measures of average and spread, including median and quartiles. Know when to add or multiply two probabilities. Use tree diagrams to calculate probabilities of combinations of independent events.	Pupils confidently use their knowledge of mathematics to develop their own alternative methods and approaches to creating solutions. Pupils select and combine known facts and problem-solving strategies to solve problems of increasing complexity. Pupils confidently convey mathematical meaning through precise and consistent use of symbols. Pupils take nothing at face value and always further examine generalisations or solutions. Pupils are able to comment constructively on the reasoning and logic of the processes employed, with the ability to suggest alternative approaches which may produce more accurate results.

Red Manglish mat: Citizenship

Reading	Writing
Pupils are developing an ability to choose their evidence precisely to support their arguments or conclusions.	Pupils effectively use a variety of sentence types and punctuation to achieve purpose and overall effect.
Pupils' ability to draw on knowledge of other sources to develop or clinch an argument is clearly developing as they have their own insights into texts after teasing out meanings and weighing up evidence. For example, they may reject an argument after exploring what is left unsaid and after comparing it to the rest of the evidence gathered.	Pupils plan the organisation of the text with the purpose in mind. Paragraphs may flow effortlessly into each other or sections may stand out for increased clarity. Openings may be linked with endings to create the echo of an argument.
Pupils show an appreciation for a writer's use of language, structure and techniques, and use their understanding of this to analyse texts for their purpose and effect. For example, pupils may use an extended metaphor of CCTV, as the eyes of the government, as a hook for the audience and compare it to a report based solely on factual evidence.	Pupils create a range of texts with distinct and original viewpoints (not necessarily their own). When pupils are making vocabulary or technique choices, they think creatively about the effect on their purpose and audience.
Pupils begin to independently analyse the context of a text, looking at its place in history and how it has been influenced by other texts to explore the viewpoint, purpose and effect on a range of audiences. For example, pupils may use Orwell's *1984* and discuss its setting, as compared to the reality of CCTV today.	Pupils use correct spelling throughout and challenge themselves with their vocabulary choices.

SILVER

Communication	Term-specific mathematics	Using and applying mathematics
Pupils are capable of using speech to explore a wide range of subjects. Planned talks are delivered to create specific effects upon different audiences. Pupils' choices of vocabulary, grammar and non-verbal features are apt and effective. Pupils can adapt easily to new audiences and purposes including a variety of group-working roles. When listening to others, pupils are able to interrogate and extend upon what is said with well-judged questions delivered in a way which extends the speaker's thinking. When creating roles, pupils make insightful choices of speech, gesture, movement and dramatic approaches with confidence. Pupils' knowledge of spoken language allows them to evaluate the meaning and impact of how they and others use and adapt language for specific purposes.	Pupils can: Suggest a problem to explore using statistical methods, frame questions and raise conjectures, and identify possible sources of bias and plan how to minimise it. Select, construct and modify (on paper and using ICT) suitable graphical representations to progress an enquiry, including frequency polygons and lines of best fit on scattergraphs. Estimate the mean, median and range of a set of grouped data and determine the modal class, selecting the statistic most appropriate to the line of enquiry. Compare two or more distributions and make inferences, using the shape of the distributions and measures of average and range. Understand relative frequency as an estimate of probability and use this to compare outcomes of an experiment, examine critically the results of a statistical enquiry and justify the choice of statistical representation in a written presentation.	Pupils are able to use their mathematically reasoned research to evaluate future solutions. For example, pupils may choose to look at different countries, exploring the crime rates and deployment of CCTV, and compare their findings to decide on how CCTV could be improved in the UK. Pupils' confidence in the application of mathematics allows them to explore connections in mathematics across a range of contexts. Pupils appreciate the difference between a mathematical argument and experimental evidence. They are able to use and present both using a wealth of presentational structures. Pupils confidently justify their findings and create effective solutions based on accurately reasoned mathematical evidence.

Red Manglish mat: Citizenship

	Reading	Writing
BRONZE	When using texts as evidence, pupils make relevant points, including summary and synthesis of information from different sources or different places in the same text.	Pupils use a full range of sentence structures and they are beginning to use them to manipulate their readers.
	Pupils' comments are securely based in textual evidence and they explore layers of meaning. For example, when exploring the connotations of bias in a newspaper article.	Pupils are confident with their use of punctuation and use it to create effects. Before proofreading, pupils may still make errors with ambitious structures but can spot these errors before redrafting.
	Pupils recognise why the writer has structured the work in a specific way to create the overall effect on the reader.	When planning, pupils make choices about the structure of the text to have specific effects on the reader. For example, if they are creating a political speech, they may choose to emphasise a specific point at the start of each new topic (e.g. 'CCTV causes fear and distrust').
	Pupils understand how the writer has used language and techniques and can trace them throughout a text to give a detailed explanation of the text as a whole. They begin to consider wider implications, layers of meaning and different audiences over different time periods when discussing this.	Pupils plan to use certain language choices and techniques to create more convincing viewpoints. They are aware of the conventions associated with a range of text types and use this information to make their text convincing.
	Pupils use the context of a text to identify the writer's intended purpose and effect. They can easily identify the viewpoint of a text and its role in the purpose and effect. For example, the writer is taking a neutral standpoint as they look from both the eyes of someone whose privacy has been invaded and the eyes of someone who has been protected by the use of CCTV.	Pupils use correct spelling throughout, including some ambitious, uncommon words. Pupils actively seek to increase their vocabulary.
	Pupils can discuss in detail how a text is affected by its context. Pupils recognise how the meaning and reception of a text can change over time and how conventions of text types can change over time.	

Communication	Term-specific mathematics	Using and applying mathematics
Pupils can explore complex ideas in a range of ways. They are able to keep talk succinct or extended upon points for greater clarity. Pupils are controlled in their planned talks and guide listeners as a result of their structure. Pupils adapt vocabulary, grammar and non-verbal features, depending upon the situation.

Pupils can engage with complex discussion, adapting to any group role and listening to a range of points before making perceptive responses. They show an awareness of the speaker's aims and extended meanings but question them further, adding more to the discussion.

Pupils are flexible in their choices of speech, gesture and movement, and can create different roles convincingly.

Pupils have a wide-ranging knowledge of spoken language features and use them to recognise spoken language choices made by others. | Pupils can:

Design a survey or experiment to capture the necessary data from one or more sources; design, trial and, if necessary, refine data collection sheets; and construct tables for large discrete and continuous sets of raw data, choosing suitable class intervals.

Design and use two-way tables.

Select, construct and modify (on paper and using ICT) pie charts for categorical data, bar charts and frequency diagrams for discrete and continuous data, as well as simple time graphs for time series and scattergraphs. They identify which are most useful in the context of the problem as well as find and record all possible mutually exclusive outcomes for single events and two successive events in a systematic way.

Know that the sum of probabilities of all mutually exclusive outcomes is 1 and use this when solving problems and communicating interpretations and results of a statistical survey, using selected tables, graphs and diagrams in support. | Pupils show confidence when identifying and solving mathematical problems.

Pupils recognise when it is sensible to order their investigations into smaller, more manageable tasks.

When presenting their findings, pupils interpret, discuss and synthesise information in a variety of mathematical forms. Their argument is effectively reasoned using symbols, diagrams, graphs and related explanatory texts, using logical argument to establish the truth of a statement. Pupils may ask the question, 'Is CCTV a waste of time?' and plan to use statistics over time to support their argument. |

Blue Manglish Mat: Citizenship

	Reading	Writing
GOLD	Pupils are selective about their use of evidence and can use quotations to back up their deductions about the text. Pupils infer meaning and deduce using examples from the text to back up their ideas. Pupils are able to identify how the text is organised and can refer to a range of features (e.g. 'Anecdotes are used in each section to provide real-life examples throughout'). Pupils are able to identify a range of language features used by the writer with some explanation (e.g. 'When it gets to the climax they speak in short sentences and quickly which makes it more tense'). Pupils can easily identify the viewpoint of a text (e.g. 'The writer is strongly against CCTV and wants to persuade the reader of their point of view'). Pupils can confidently identify text types for different purposes, such as leaflets, newspapers and diary entries. When identifying the main purpose of a text, pupils are able to comment on how the context of a text can affect the meaning. For example, a text written by someone whose attacker was caught on CCTV may be biased.	Pupils use a full range of sentence structures for different purposes. Pupils can use a full range of punctuation correctly. They may make mistakes when attempting ambitious structures (e.g. 'Unlike countries with little or no human rights we, the people of Britain, are given many freedoms, we are able to choose what we say and how we say it.' Here the first use of commas for parenthesis is correct, but the second should be a semicolon as both sides of the comma could stand alone as sentences). Pupils plan their paragraphs to create a coherent and logical structure. Their openings and endings are effective. Connectives are used throughout to signal changes in time or message (e.g. therefore, however, unlike, before, meanwhile). Pupils plan their viewpoint and make vocabulary choices with the purpose and audience in mind. They are convincing. Pupils spell all common words correctly and no longer make mistakes with homophones. Pupils use dictionaries effectively to find new spellings. More complicated spellings may be incorrect (e.g. outrageous, exaggerated, announcing, parallel). Pupils should be provided with challenging topic-specific vocabulary lists.

Communication	Term-specific mathematics	Using and applying mathematics
Pupils elaborate on points to express and explain relevant ideas and feelings. Pupils plan what they say to make their meaning clear and to have an effect upon, as well as to engage, the listener.	Pupils can:	Pupils independently identify mathematical problems and are able to obtain the necessary information to come up with solutions. For example, pupils may choose to compare the crime rates in areas before and after the installation of CCTV and work out the probability of crime rates rising if CCTV was taken away.
	Ask questions, plan how to answer them and collect the data required in terms of probability.	
	Select methods based on equally likely outcomes and experimental evidence, as appropriate.	
Pupils deliberately match vocabulary, grammar and non-verbal features to their audience, purpose and context.	Understand and use the probability scale from 0 to 1.	
	Understand and use the mean of discrete data and compare two simple distributions, using the range and one of mode, median or mean.	Pupils independently check results, considering whether these are reasonable.
When listening to others, pupils recognise implicit meanings and develop on what has been said with comments and questions.		
		Pupils apply their new learning from mathematics lessons to new investigations from a range of contexts.
Pupils are able to take on a range of roles in groups effectively and are able to take a leading role in shaping discussions, as well as developing characters beyond themselves through deliberate choices of speech, movement and gesture.	Understand that different outcomes may result from repeating an experiment.	
	Interpret graphs and diagrams (including pie charts) and draw conclusions, and create and interpret line graphs where the intermediate values have meaning.	Pupils are confident when speaking using newly acquired mathematical language and when interpreting symbols and diagrams to explain their own logical reasoning of problems.
Pupils are able to explain features of their own and others' language use, showing understanding of effect of varying language for different purposes and situations.		

Blue Manglish Mat: Citizenship

	Reading	Writing
SILVER	When using the text to support their ideas, pupils can refer to points in the text to back up their ideas but often paraphrase rather than make clear selections. When inferring meaning, pupils are able to refer to points in the text to explain why they think their ideas about it are correct. Pupils are able to recognise why a text has been ordered in the way it has. For example, the writer uses bullet points to highlight their main points, or uses a real-life example first to set the scene. Pupils are able to pick out word classes and techniques, such as verbs or alliteration, and explain why the writer has chosen them. For example, they may say that a writer has chosen to use the adjectives 'invasive' and 'intrusive' when they explain how people feel about CCTV. Pupils can comment on the intended effect of a text on a reader. For example, they may say that a newspaper report only describes the negative aspects because the writer wants the reader to agree that CCTV is bad. Pupils can recognise features common to different text types. For example, pupils will identify the presentational features of a newspaper report and know that a diary entry is presented differently. When identifying the main purpose of a text, pupils understand that writers have their own opinions and that it is important to know where a text is set and who wrote it.	Pupils are beginning to use complex sentences, as well as simple and compound sentences, and they are learning to use subordinate clauses (e.g. 'Before discussing the topic in more depth, let me tell you the story of Martha Jones and her brush with CCTV'). Pupils write in the correct tense with occasional errors. Pupils can use full stops, capital letters, question marks, exclamation marks and speech marks without making mistakes. Pupils can use commas in lists and are learning to use them to indicate subordinate clauses. Pupils plan topics for each of their paragraphs and begin each paragraph with a topic sentence. Ideas are in a logical order. Sentences are connected with more varied connectives, such as 'also' or 'then', but one or more can often be overused. Pupils can create a believable viewpoint and match it to their purpose and readers, although they are not always consistent. They elaborate on ideas by using expanded noun and adverbial phrases (e.g. 'The prying, invasive eyes of CCTV'). Pupils choose their vocabulary deliberately to match their purpose but are not overly ambitious with their choices. Pupils' spelling of common words is correct. This includes spelling rules for suffixes such as adding -ly and changing tense. Homophones may still be confused. Provide pupils with a unit-specific word bank to support spelling of new vocabulary.

Communication	Term-specific mathematics	Using and applying mathematics
Pupils are able to speak in extended turns to express their ideas and feelings. Pupils have given thought to how their listener may respond before they speak. As a listener, they consider what has been said and comment upon it, showing understanding.

Pupils recognise that vocabulary, grammar and non-verbal features should be adapted, depending on the purpose and audience.

Pupils understand the purpose of different roles in groups and show that they have attempted to adapt their talk to suit the needs of their situation.

Pupils are able to create different roles and begin to make deliberate choices of speech, gesture, language and movement. | Pupils can:

Collect and record discrete group data, where appropriate, in equal class intervals.

Continue to use Venn and Carroll diagrams to record their sorting and classifying of information.

Construct and interpret frequency diagrams and simple line graphs.

Understand and use the mode and range to describe sets of data. | Pupils are able to develop their own strategies for solving simple problems.

Pupils can apply newly acquired mathematics to practical contexts. For example, they have just learned to sort and classify information and so may decide to sort areas using CCTV and their crime rates into groups. They may also choose to use the mode to explore where most crimes happen in relation to CCTV.

Pupils always present information and results in a clear and organised way. |

Blue Manglish Mat: Citizenship

	Reading	Writing
BRONZE	Pupils can read a text fluently and use their understanding of phonetics to read unfamiliar words out loud. They can work out the meanings of new words.	Pupils' sentences are often basic. For example, using only simple sentences (e.g. 'CCTV is a problem') or compound sentences (e.g. 'CCTV is a problem and people don't like it)'.
	Pupils can recognise and retell the main points of the text.	Pupils will most commonly use 'and', 'but' and 'so' to connect sentences.
	Pupils can use the text as an example but will often retell the story of the text rather than using it to support their own ideas.	Pupils do not always use the right tense for their writing and may even switch between tenses without any purpose.
	Pupils can recognise word classes, such as adjectives, verbs, nouns and pronouns, within a text but do not comment on why they are used.	Pupils can use capital letters, full stops, exclamation marks and question marks in the right places.
	Pupils can recognise why a writer has written the text and can infer meaning. For example, in a newspaper report about CCTV pupils may recognise that the writer is biased as they use only negative examples.	Pupils will order their text logically but may not use clear paragraphs. Links between ideas are made within the writing but some ideas may appear disjointed.
	Pupils can recognise differences and similarities between texts and their writers' viewpoints by inferring simple meanings. Pupils understand that some newspaper articles may be biased.	Pupils can adopt a viewpoint. For example, if they are asked to write an example of pro-war propaganda, they will use positive vocabulary. They may expand on their nouns with simple adjectives (e.g. 'Scary CCTV is horrible').
		Pupils may need support with setting out their work to match the style of the genre.
		Pupils use words that are appropriate to the set task but are not ambitious in their vocabulary choices.
		Common words are spelled correctly and unfamiliar words are often written phonetically. Pupils may need support with spelling and should be given unit-specific word banks. Homophones are likely to cause confusion (e.g. there, their, they're; too, two, to).

Communication	Term-specific mathematics	Using and applying mathematics
Pupils can present how they feel to one another by taking turns in extended speaking about a topic, while maintaining eye contact and using gesticulation to further express their feelings. Pupils show that they are listening to other speakers' main ideas by making comments and suggestions. Pupils try out different roles in groups and attempt to take on different viewpoints or roles by adapting what they say and how they say it.	Pupils can: Gather information. Construct bar charts and pictograms, where the symbol represents a group of units. Use Venn and Carroll diagrams to record their sorting and classifying of information. Extract and interpret information presented in simple tables, lists, bar charts and pictograms.	Pupils are able to select the mathematics they want to use, from a range provided by the teacher, to solve mathematical problems. They may choose to use a pie chart over a bar graph to better represent how CCTV has developed over time. Pupils try out different simple mathematical approaches to find ways of overcoming problems. Pupils begin to organise their work logically and check their results are accurate. Pupils may use a calculator to check that survey results have been added up correctly. Pupils are able to use and interpret mathematical symbols and diagrams. For example, pupils may use graphs representing the effects of CCTV.

English and statistics

This English lesson would be the first lesson taught to pupils in this unit of work. Last term, the focus of maths lessons was the use of statistics in problem-solving. As the curriculum was collaboratively planned, English teachers would have worked with maths teachers during the previous term and would be aware of the mathematical abilities of their pupils. They would also be informed about the topics covered and the outcomes reached. The Manglish mats for this half-term can, once again, be found at the end of this lesson (pages 100–111).

Connect

Any successful fictional team that has been depicted in film could be used for the purpose of this lesson. Pupils probably won't have seen the movie you choose so, not to waste any time as pupils await your arrival, display mugshots of the main characters on the wall outside the classroom, along with their names and details about them.

When pupils enter the room, you could play the film's theme music or trailer to set the scene (these are usually available online). On the board (just like outside) are mugshots of the team members alongside the question, 'Do you recognise yourself in any of these characters?' to connect the pupils' learning directly to the lesson.

Lesson outcome

What? To be able to interpret a director's intentions.
How? Through analysis of the film trailer for clues, using effective communication and recognising the factors involved in characterisation.
Why? To be able to mirror and build upon a director's techniques when creating our own characters.

New information

This English lesson has been created to embed mathematical skills from the previous term and give pupils a purpose in a different context. The outcome of this lesson is to interpret a writer's intentions though their characterisations, but they will be doing this using frequency analysis and problem-solving.

Pupils are set by mathematical ability and are seated in teams of four. They can watch the trailer on their smartphones, tablets or desktop computers or as a whole class on the main whiteboard. Pupils are told that their challenge is to work out what the director is trying to tell us about the characters.

As they watch, they make a simple tally of how many times each character appears (that's why it would be better on a device that the group can control, so they can stop and start the trailer at will). The frequency of character appearances is a starting point, but they are challenged to look out for more possibilities to analyse.

Pupils are provided with the following guidance to help focus their efforts on success:

MATHEMATICS, READING AND COMMUNICATION

Blue Gold

Mathematics:

Have you compared two sets of results using the range and one of the mode, median or mean?

Can you consider different approaches to the problem based on your results?

Reading:

Have you used specific quotes from the trailer as part of your response?

Communication:

Have you demonstrated confidence when discussing your ideas?

Are you aware of your body language (e.g. eye contact, tone of voice)?

Have you been paying close attention to what others say?

Do you ask questions to develop ideas?

Blue Silver

Mathematics:

Have you collected data in a clear frequency table?

Could you use the mode and range to describe the data you have gathered?

Reading:

Which parts of the trailer prove your explanation of characterisation is correct?

Communication:

How are you showing confidence in your group?

How can you demonstrate you are developing ideas thoughtfully and conveying your opinions clearly?

Have you listened carefully in discussions?

What questions have you asked that added to others' ideas?

Blue Bronze

Mathematics:

What is the information you have gathered telling you?

Can you create a diagram to explain your findings in a clear, straightforward way?

Reading:

Can you describe the director's intentions?

Communication:

Can you explain why writers choose specific words?

How have you shown confidence while discussing your ideas in your group?

Have you asked your team members questions?

Search for meaning

From the initial question, gold level pupils would recognise the most frequent character and may draw the conclusion that they are the leader and, as another character appears the least, that they may be insignificant. However, after consulting their success criteria, they would see that by sticking to this conclusion they could only remain working at a bronze level. They need to approach the problem from different angles to come up with a range of ideas to compare. This group use the criteria for communication to determine how they can reach a decision on their next steps. They would talk confidently and ask questions to develop each other's ideas.

Have ideas ready to prompt bronze pupils, but do not force your ideas on them. Allow them space to discover the art of characterisation for themselves. If necessary, you could prompt them with simple ideas, such as cards stating 'facial expression', 'movement', 'position on screen', 'shouting vs. quiet' or 'smiling vs. serious'. The chances are that, with their amazing imaginations, pupils will come up with better ideas than yours!

Demonstrate

Pupils should now demonstrate their findings to the rest of the class by creating a movie trailer of their own. As directors, they are increasing their confidence in responding in that role as well as interpreting the data they have gathered. Pupils cannot just act foolish and hope to achieve gold. They must put themselves in the mind of a director and make decisions based on their understanding of his or her creation.

For example, one group decides to begin with a close-up of their main character and have them appear in every subsequent shot slightly higher than the other characters, to represent their importance within the group. They have recognised from their analysis that, although not present in every shot, the director of the movie always had their main character appear in the highest position in the scene. They used their reasoning, based on their results, to include this as part of their sequence.

Review

The pupils have been given the opportunity to practise frequency analysis in a subject where they would not ordinarily find maths; it has been used purposefully to help them achieve their outcome. Imagine that these pupils are now leaving English and heading into a PE lesson. The next lesson idea demonstrates how the Manglish PE lesson endorses their ability to apply problem-solving and analysis skills.

The following two tables are the red and blue Manglish mats used by English teachers to plan and differentiate over this half-term.

Red Manglish Mat: English

	Reading	Writing
GOLD	Pupils have the ability to develop a clear critical stance on any text presented to them. They use texts to develop coherent interpretations of texts and issues.	Sentence structures are used imaginatively and with precision to have specific effects throughout the text.
	Pupils are able to make imaginative, insightful evaluations as a result of their wealth of knowledge of text types, purposes, audiences, language, structure and techniques. Pupils' insights are always well supported by precise references and wider textual knowledge.	Structural devices, language and techniques manipulate readers depending upon the purpose of the text.
	Pupils fully appreciate the overall effect of texts of various different genres over various time periods. They show clear understanding and critical evaluation of writers' purposes and viewpoints and how these are articulated throughout the text.	Pupils have an original style and, thanks to a wide-ranging knowledge of text types and purposes, can manipulate different genres successfully. A range of viewpoints can be skilfully adopted with ease.
	Pupils are independently critical of texts and their origins. They analyse and evaluate texts to determine for themselves how texts relate to particular contexts and traditions and how they may be received over time.	Correct spelling and effective, imaginatively chosen, ambitious vocabulary is used throughout.

Communication	Term-specific mathematics	Using and applying mathematics
Pupils demonstrate that they can make creative selections from a wide repertoire of strategies and conventions to meet varied speaking and listening challenges. Pupils consciously adapt their vocabulary, grammar and non-verbal features to any situation, including group-working roles, speeches, debates and drama. Pupils are able to sustain concentrated and sensitive listening; they respond with flexibility to creatively develop the ideas of others. Pupils can exploit a range of dramatic approaches and techniques creatively to create complex and believable roles. Pupils have an excellent knowledge of spoken language features and continually reflect on their own and others' choices.	Pupils can: Estimate and find the median, quartiles and interquartile range for large data sets, including using a cumulative frequency diagram. Compare two or more distributions and make inferences using the shape of the distributions and measures of average and spread, including median and quartiles. Know when to add or multiply two probabilities. Use tree diagrams to calculate probabilities of combinations of independent events.	Pupils confidently use their knowledge of mathematics to develop their own alternative methods and approaches to creating solutions. Pupils select and combine known facts and problem-solving strategies to solve problems of increasing complexity. Pupils confidently convey mathematical meaning through precise and consistent use of symbols. Pupils take nothing at face value and always further examine generalisations or solutions. Pupils are able to comment constructively on the reasoning and logic of the processes employed, with the ability to suggest alternative approaches which may produce more accurate results.

Red Manglish Mat: English

	Reading	Writing
SILVER	Pupils are developing an ability to choose their evidence precisely to support their arguments or conclusions.	Pupils effectively use a variety of sentence types and punctuation to achieve purpose and overall effect.
	Pupils' ability to draw on knowledge of other sources to develop or clinch an argument is clearly developing, as they have their own insights into texts after teasing out meanings and weighing up evidence. For example, they may reject an argument after exploring what is left unsaid and after comparing it to the rest of the evidence gathered.	Pupils plan the organisation of the text with the purpose in mind. Paragraphs may flow effortlessly into each other or sections may stand out for increased clarity. Openings may be linked with endings to create the echo of an argument.
	Pupils show an appreciation for a writer's use of language, structure and techniques, and use their understanding of this to analyse texts for their purpose and effect.	Pupils create a range of texts with distinct and original viewpoints (not necessarily their own). When pupils are making vocabulary or technique choices, they think creatively about the effect on their purpose and audience.
	Pupils begin to independently analyse the context of a text, looking at its place in history and how it has been influenced by other texts to explore the viewpoint, purpose and effect on a range of audiences.	Pupils use correct spelling throughout and challenge themselves with their vocabulary choices.

Communication	Term-specific mathematics	Using and applying mathematics
Pupils are capable of using talk to explore a wide range of subjects. Planned talks are delivered to create specific effects on different audiences. Pupils' choices of vocabulary, grammar and non-verbal features are apt and effective. Pupils can adapt easily to new audiences and purposes, including a variety of group-working roles. When listening to others, pupils are able to interrogate and extend upon what is said with well-judged questions delivered in a way which extends the speaker's thinking. When creating roles, pupils make insightful choices of speech, gesture, movement and dramatic approaches with confidence. Pupil's knowledge of spoken language allows them to evaluate the meaning and impact of how they and others use and adapt language for specific purposes.	Pupils can: Suggest a problem to explore using statistical methods, frame questions and raise conjectures, and identify possible sources of bias and plan how to minimise it. Select, construct and modify (on paper and using ICT) suitable graphical representations to progress an enquiry, including frequency polygons and lines of best fit on scattergraphs. Estimate the mean, median and range of a set of grouped data and determine the modal class, selecting the statistic most appropriate to the line of enquiry. Compare two or more distributions and make inferences using the shape of the distributions and measures of average and range. Understand relative frequency as an estimate of probability and use this to compare outcomes of an experiment, examine critically the results of a statistical enquiry and justify the choice of statistical representation in written presentation.	Pupils are able to use their mathematically reasoned research to evaluate future solutions. For example, they may be able to state that a character's frequency in a trailer determines their importance in the film. Pupils' confidence in the application of mathematics allows them to explore connections in mathematics across a range of contexts. Pupils appreciate the difference between a mathematical argument and experimental evidence. They are able to use and present both using a wealth of presentational structures. Pupils confidently justify their findings and create effective solutions based on accurately reasoned mathematical evidence.

Red Manglish Mat: English

	Reading	Writing
BRONZE	When using texts as evidence, pupils make relevant points, including summary and synthesis of information from different sources or different places in the same text. Pupils' comments are securely based in textual evidence and they explore layers of meaning. For example, when exploring connotations in a poem or advertisement. Pupils recognise why the writer has structured the work in a specific way, to create an overall effect on the reader. Pupils understand how the writer has used language and techniques and can trace them throughout a text to give a detailed explanation of the text as a whole. They begin to consider wider implications, layers of meaning and different audiences over different time periods when discussing this. Pupils use the context of a text to identify the writer's intended purpose and effect. They can easily identify the viewpoint of a text and its role in the purpose and effect. For example, the writer has chosen to use the first-person to engage personally with their reader. Pupils can discuss in detail how a text is affected by its context. Pupils recognise how the meaning and reception of a text can change over time and how conventions of text types can change over time.	Pupils use a full range of sentence structures and they are beginning to use them to manipulate their readers. Pupils are confident with their use of punctuation and use it to create effects. Before proofreading, pupils may still make errors with ambitious structures but can spot these errors before redrafting. When planning, pupils make choices about the structure of the text to have specific effects on the reader. For example, if they are creating a persuasive argument, they may choose to open and end with an effective choice of rhetorical question. Pupils plan to use certain language choices and techniques to create more convincing viewpoints. They are aware of the conventions associated with a range of text types and use this information to make their text convincing. Pupils use correct spelling throughout, including some ambitious, uncommon words. Pupils actively seek to increase their vocabulary.

Communication	Term-specific mathematics	Using and applying mathematics
Pupils can explore complex ideas in a range of ways. They are able to keep talk succinct or extend upon points for greater clarity. Pupils are controlled in their planned talks and guide listeners as a result of their structure. Pupils adapt vocabulary, grammar and non-verbal features depending upon the situation.	Pupils can: Design a survey or experiment to capture the necessary data from one or more sources; design, trial and, if necessary, refine data collection sheets; construct tables for large, discrete and continuous sets of raw data, choosing suitable class intervals; and design and use two-way tables.	Pupils show confidence when identifying and solving mathematical problems. Pupils recognise when it is sensible to order their investigations into smaller, more manageable tasks. For example, when exploring the representation of characters, they may choose to approach one character at a time before reviewing the overall results.
Pupils can engage with complex discussion, adapting to any group role and listening to a range of points before making perceptive responses. They show an awareness of the speaker's aims and extended meanings but question them further adding more to the discussion.	Select, construct and modify (on paper and using ICT) pie charts for categorical data, bar charts and frequency diagrams for discrete and continuous data simple time graphs for time series scatter graphs.	When presenting their findings, pupils interpret, discuss and synthesise information in a variety of mathematical forms. Their argument is effectively reasoned using symbols, diagrams, graphs and related explanatory texts using logical argument to establish the truth of a statement. For example, they will use data gathered during an investigation to highlight their final argument and present it in a way which makes their findings clear to the reader, such as stating the character's appearances as percentages.
Pupils are flexible in their choices of speech, gesture and movement, and can create different roles convincingly.	Identify the most useful tools and methods for a given problem, as well as find and record all possible outcomes for events in a systematic way.	
Pupils have a wide-ranging knowledge of spoken language features and use them to recognise spoken language choices made by others.	Know that the sum of probabilities of all mutually exclusive outcomes is 1 and use this when solving problems.	
	Communicate interpretations and results of a statistical survey using selected tables, graphs and diagrams in support.	

Blue Manglish Mat: English

	Reading	Writing
GOLD	Pupils are selective about their use of evidence and can use quotations to back up their deductions about the text.	Pupils use a full range of sentence structures for different purposes.
	Pupils infer meaning and deduce using examples from the text to back up their ideas.	Pupils can use a full range of punctuation correctly. They may make mistakes when attempting ambitious structures.
	Pupils are able to identify how the text is organised and can refer to a range of features (e.g. 'Each section starts with a question as if he's answering the crowd').	Pupils plan their paragraphs to create a coherent and logical structure. Their openings and endings are effective. Connectives are used throughout to signal changes in time or message (e.g. therefore, however, unlike, before, meanwhile).
	Pupils are able to identify a range of language features used by the writer with some explanation (e.g. 'When it gets to the climax they speak in short sentences and quickly which makes it more tense').	Pupils plan their viewpoint and make vocabulary choices with the purpose and audience in mind. They are convincing.
	Pupils can easily identify the viewpoint of a text (e.g. 'The writer is creating a tense atmosphere as they want the reader to feel unsure about this character').	Pupils spell all common words correctly and no longer make mistakes with homophones. Pupils use dictionaries effectively to find new spellings. More complicated spellings may be incorrect (e.g. outrageous, exaggerated, announcing, parallel). Pupils should be provided with challenging topic-specific vocabulary lists.
	Pupils can confidently identify text types for different purposes, such as leaflets, newspapers and diary entries.	
	When identifying the main purpose of a text, pupils are able to comment on how the context of a text can affect the meaning (e.g. 'A text written by a parent may be more biased about their child than a text written by a newspaper columnist').	

Communication	Term-specific mathematics	Using and applying mathematics
Pupils elaborate on points to express and explain relevant ideas and feelings. Pupils plan what they say to make their meaning clear and to have an effect upon, as well as to engage, the listener. Pupils deliberately match vocabulary, grammar and non-verbal features to their audience, purpose and context. When listening to others, pupils recognise implicit meanings and develop upon what has been said with comments and questions. Pupils are able to take on a range of roles in groups effectively and are able to take a leading role in shaping discussions, as well as developing characters beyond themselves through deliberate choices of speech, movement and gesture. Pupils are able to explain features of their own and others' language use, showing understanding of the effect of varying language for different purposes and situations.	Pupils can: Ask questions, plan how to answer them and collect the data required in terms of probability, and select methods based on equally likely outcomes and experimental evidence, as appropriate. Understand and use the probability scale from 0 to 1. Understand and use the mean of discrete data and compare two simple distributions, using the range and one of mode, median or mean. Understand that different outcomes may result from repeating an experiment, and interpret graphs and diagrams, including pie charts. Draw conclusions and create and interpret line graphs where the intermediate values have meaning.	Pupils independently identify mathematical problems and are able to obtain the necessary information to come up with solutions. For example, pupils identify that directors are able to manipulate the audience and apply rules of ratio to the number of character appearances. Pupils independently check results, considering whether these are reasonable. Pupils apply their new learning from mathematics lessons to new investigations from a range of contexts. Pupils are confident when speaking using newly acquired mathematical language and interpreting symbols and diagrams to explain their own logical reasoning of problems.

Blue Manglish Mat: English

Reading	Writing
SILVER	

<table>
<tr><th>Reading</th><th>Writing</th></tr>
<tr><td>

When using the text to support their ideas, pupils can refer to points in the text to back up their ideas but often paraphrase rather than make clear selections.

When inferring meaning, pupils are able to refer to points in the text to explain why they think their ideas about it are correct.

Pupils are able to recognise why a text has been ordered in the way it has. For example, the writer uses bullet points to highlight their main points.

Pupils are able to pick out word classes and techniques, such as verbs or alliteration, and explain why the writer has chosen them. For example, they may say that a writer has chosen to use the adjectives 'bright' and 'sunny' as they have positive connotations.

Pupils can comment on the intended effect of a text on a reader. For example, they may say that a newspaper report only describes the negative events because the writer wants the reader to sense the negativity and side with their point of view.

Pupils can recognise features common to different text types. For example, pupils will recognise the presentational features of a newspaper report and know that a diary entry is presented differently.

When identifying the main purpose of a text, pupils understand that writers have their own opinions and that it is important to know where a text is set and who wrote it.

</td><td>

Pupils are beginning to use complex sentences, as well as simple and compound sentences, and they are learning to use subordinate clauses.

Pupils write in the correct tense with occasional errors.

Pupils can use full stops, capital letters, question marks, exclamation marks and speech marks without making mistakes. Pupils can use commas in lists and are learning to use them to indicate subordinate clauses.

Pupils plan topics for each of their paragraphs and begin each paragraph with a topic sentence. Ideas are in a logical order. Sentences are connected with more varied connectives, such as 'also' or 'then', but one or more can often be overused.

Pupils can create a believable viewpoint and match it to their purpose and readers, although they are not always consistent. They elaborate on ideas by using expanded noun and adverbial phrases.

Pupils choose their vocabulary deliberately to match their purpose but are not overly ambitious with their choices.

Pupils' spelling of common words is correct. This includes spelling rules for suffixes such as adding -ly and changing tense. Homophones may still be confused. Provide pupils with a unit-specific word bank to support spelling of new vocabulary.

</td></tr>
</table>

Communication	Term-specific mathematics	Using and applying mathematics
Pupils are able to speak in extended turns to express their ideas and feelings. Pupils have given thought to how their listener may respond before they speak. As a listener, they consider what has been said and comment upon it showing understanding.	Pupils can: Collect and record discrete data. Group data, where appropriate, in equal class intervals. Continue to use Venn and Carroll diagrams to record their sorting and classifying of information. Construct and interpret frequency diagrams and simple line graphs. Understand and use the mode and range to describe sets of data.	Pupils are able to develop their own strategies for solving simple problems. They may choose to use a tally chart and eventually convert it into a pie chart when gathering and presenting data, as they feel this is the most effective way to investigate the problem.
Pupils recognise that vocabulary, grammar and non-verbal features should be adapted, depending on the purpose and audience.		Pupils can apply newly acquired mathematics to practical contexts. For example, they have just learned to work out percentages in mathematics lessons and so see that they can turn survey findings into percentages.
Pupils understand the purpose of different roles in groups and show that they have attempted to adapt their talk to suit the needs of their situation.		Pupils always present information and results in a clear and organised way.
Pupils are able to create different roles and begin to make deliberate choices of speech, gesture, language and movement.		

Blue Manglish Mat: English

	Reading	Writing
BRONZE	Pupils can read a text fluently and use their understanding of phonetics to read unfamiliar words out loud. They can work out the meanings of new words. Pupils can recognise and retell the main points of the text. Pupils can use the text as an example but will often retell the story of the text rather than using it to support their own ideas. Pupils can recognise word classes, such as adjectives, verbs, nouns, pronouns, within a text but do not comment on why they are used. Pupils can recognise why a writer has written the text and can infer meaning. For example, pupils can state that a poem is positive because it uses lots of positive words. Pupils can recognise differences and similarities between texts and their writers' viewpoints by inferring simple meanings.	Pupils' sentences are often basic. For example, only using simple sentences or compound sentences. Pupils will most commonly use 'and', 'but' and 'so' to connect sentences. Pupils do not always use the right tense for their writing and may even switch between tenses without any purpose. Pupils can use capital letters, full stops, exclamation marks and question marks in the right places. Pupils will order their text logically but may not use clear paragraphs. There are links between ideas made within the writing but some ideas may appear disjointed. Pupils can adopt a viewpoint. For example, they can create a text that has a very positive or a very negative message. Pupils may need support with setting out their work to match the style of the genre. Pupils use words that are appropriate to the set task but are not ambitious in their vocabulary choices. Common words are spelled correctly and unfamiliar words are often written phonetically. Pupils may need support with spelling and should be given unit-specific word banks. Homophones are likely to cause confusion (e.g. there, their, they're; too, two, to).

Communication	Term-specific mathematics	Using and applying mathematics
Pupils can present how they feel to one another by taking turns in extended speaking about a topic, while maintaining eye contact and using gesticulation to further express their feelings. Pupils show that they are listening to other speakers' main ideas by making comments and suggestions. Pupils try out different roles in groups and attempt to take on different viewpoints or roles by adapting what they say and how they say it.	Pupils can: Gather information. Construct bar charts and pictograms, where the symbol represents a group of units. Use Venn and Carroll diagrams to record their sorting and classifying of information. Extract and interpret information presented in simple tables, lists, bar charts and pictograms.	Pupils are able to select the mathematics they want to use, from a range provided by the teacher, to solve mathematical problems. They may choose to use a pie chart over a bar graph to better represent their investigation's findings. Pupils try out different simple mathematical approaches to find ways of overcoming problems. Pupils begin to organise their work logically and check their results are accurate. Pupils may use a calculator to check that survey results have been added up correctly. Pupils are able to use and interpret mathematical symbols and diagrams. For example, pupils will use +, = or -, or simple bar graphs and pie charts.

Physical education, statistics and communication

The big picture for this half-term is Going for Gold. Pupils are using self-gathered data to enhance their physical skills. Pupils are revisiting statistics in their maths lessons and will be putting this learning into practice today to become athletes worthy of a gold medal. The PE teachers have also been working alongside the English department to spot worthwhile opportunities for reading, writing and communication in this very practical subject.

Time is precious and even more so when you are attempting such an ambitious amalgamation of PE, reading, writing, communication and maths, as we are about to see, so this teacher had carefully divided the lesson timings as follows:

Connect: (5 minutes) This will take place in the changing rooms. Pupils are reading a poster and responding to a question as they change for the lesson. This activity promotes reading skills as well as preparing pupils for their warm-up so as to avoid wasting any learning time.

Warm-up: (5–10 minutes)

New information: (5 minutes) A teacher-led explanation of the equipment ensues and rules and expectations are explored. Pupils should fully understand the outcome of exploring the answers to 'What methods could we use to improve coordination?' before moving on to the exploration. Pupils need to know their purpose (to develop methods to improve coordination) and what they should do to achieve their purpose – experiment using mathematical skills and the equipment provided as well as learning new subject-specific vocabulary and improving communication. They are divided into groups.

Search for meaning: (20 minutes) Pupils are recording findings, discussing solutions, experimenting with ideas resulting from their observations, trying out the ideas, and using mathematical skills and communication to learn about physical education concepts.

Pupil reflection time: (5 minutes) Individually, pupils need to reflect upon what they have found out. They can discuss this with their teammates for support, but the expectation is that everyone needs to have an answer to:

'What methods could we use to improve coordination?'

Demonstrate: (10 minutes) Pupils are paired up with someone from another group to discuss the answer to the question. As they are discussing the answer, they can also stretch to cool down. The teacher circulates and takes notes of any misconceptions and decides on the teaching needs for subsequent sessions

Get changed

Lesson outcome

What? To research strategies to help improve our coordination.

How? Using effective new vocabulary as well as trial, error and learning from our mistakes.

Why? To know how to improve physical skill and learn how, through observation and simple adjustments, we can become awesome athletes!

Connect the learning and pupil review

First, pupils need to get changed ready for their workout. As they are changing, ask the pupils to go to the section of the changing room set out for their working-at level – using the central Manglish data, the teacher has allocated the pupils changing spaces. At approximately eye level for the pupils, the teacher places the Limber Bob posters (see next page) on the wall, making sure to place enough around so that pupils can read them easily as they change.

The poster is not entirely new information – pupils already have an understanding of the importance of a warm-up. They are reviewing this understanding and, in their responses, may add information that is not necessarily on the poster.

The posters are all the same; the differentiation comes from the questions. You need not separate pupils into sections of the changing room if you'd prefer not to. You could either let pupils know their working-at levels before the lesson and have the questions ready for them to pick up on the way in, allowing pupils to choose their own level of challenge as they enter (note differentiation by choice could result in some pupils not challenging themselves enough or choosing a level that does not allow them to achieve success, so you would need to monitor their choices) or, of course, you could

LOOSEN UP WITH LIMBER BOB

LIMBER UP

**Four deep breaths,
Raising your arms up.
This feels great;
We are limbering up!
Nice deep breaths,
In and out slow,
Our engines are start-
ing;
Off we go!**

LIMBER UP

**Roll your shoulders back;
This feels great!
Do that for the count of eight.
Once, Bob forgot to do this move;
His angry doctor did not approve!
Bob injured his poorly neck;
He won't forget again,
You bet!**

RHYTHMIC LIMBERING

**Doing this move
Will warm you good.
To do it properly
You should
Lift each knee
Up to your waist;
Do it slow
Not in haste.
Do it three times
to a count of eight;
Hope by now
You're feeling great!**

RHYTHMIC LIMBERING

**Our blood circulation is going up;
Time to put your arms right up.
Heels go forward, eight times
three,
Nice deep breaths,
Keep up with me.
Now we are feeling really warm
One more thing
To avoid muscles being torn
Jog on the spot
Thanks a lot
For taking part.**

BOB'S TOP REASONS FOR WARMING UP

WARMING UP REDUCES THE POTENTIAL FOR INJURY

INCREASING THE TEMPERATURE OF THE BODY MAKES MUSCLES MORE FLEXIBLE

YOUR BODY NEEDS TO BE MENTALLY READY FOR A WORKOUT

YOUR HEART RATE WILL INCREASE STEADILY READY TO BE PUSHED FURTHER (BURNING CALORIES) DURING YOUR WORKOUT.

display the questions under the posters in the sections allocated to different level pupils.

Below are examples of questions that could be asked for each level and the quality of responses that should be accepted.

> **Blue Gold question:** What should happen to your heart rate during a warm-up? How is this different from a workout? Use evidence from the poster to support your answer.

This question allows pupils to demonstrate an understanding of warm-ups (a necessity in our current expectations of teaching PE) as well as practise reading skills by extracting quotations at a **Blue Gold** level, thus supporting their literacy (see the PE Manglish mat on pages 130–131 for level criteria). The teacher must expect a direct quotation from the text and a full sentence response.

A good quality answer would look like this:

> Your heart rate should 'increase steadily' during a warm-up. This is different to the actual workout as the leaflet states that your heart rate will be 'pushed further' during the main workout. This is so that calories are being burned. By warming up before a workout, the body temperature is able to slowly rise, preparing your body for the workout.

> **Blue Silver question:** What exercises are involved in limbering up? What is the next part of the warm-up, after limbering up, called and why do we do this? Point out which parts of the poster prove this.

This question will allow pupils to demonstrate reading skills appropriate to their working-at level while also showing they can explain the basic safety involved in warming up.

A good quality answer would look like this:

> To limber up, you begin by taking deep breaths and raising both your arms up in the air. It says in the first box that you should do this slowly. You also need

to roll your shoulders back to loosen them. In the second box, it says that you should do this eight times. If you don't do this, you could get injured because the text says Bob was injured when he forgot to do this. After limbering up you move onto rhythmic limbering which warms your body up slowly ready for your workout.

Blue Bronze question: Why do you think Bob was once injured? What does he always need to do to make sure it does not happen again?

This question allows pupils to read the text and show that they have understood it; it also allows them to show that they can describe why warming up is important.

A good quality answer will look like this:

Bob was injured because he forgot to warm up properly before he began his exercise. To avoid injuring himself again he should start his warm-up by limbering up, taking deep breaths and rolling his shoulders and then move onto rhythmic limbering to make sure he is nice and warm before his main workout.

Once pupils are ready, they could complete this warm-up in their groups. Remembering that **Blue Gold** pupils should be able to 'plan, organise and lead their own activities' (the **Blue Silver** pupils should be working towards this too), each week selected pupils could research a new technique and lead the team in their warm-up. If they can also add to Bob's warm-up chant to help implement their new ideas, they are continuing to practise text creation skills at home – bonus! This will leave the teacher free to focus on the **Blue Bronze** group and ensuring that they warm up safely.

New information

Equipment required:

A set of cones per team

A ball

The word wall presentation (an interactive white board would be best so that pupils can clearly see it and use it whenever necessary)

Recording equipment – one per team (their camera phones will do but it is better if you have flip camcorders, laptops or similar)

A stopwatch

Various graph templates to record the results of the tests

Paper and pens

The main activity consists of pupils dribbling a ball through a set of cones. The teacher explains that the aim of the test is to work as a team to discover ways that we can improve our coordination. They must learn from each other, recording their findings and using the results to make improvements. Make sure that all pupils are confident with the rules before they begin experimenting.

Pupils' groups will need to be arranged so that each group has at least one stronger member – this will act as a model of good practice. Three is a great number for a team, but any more than five may hinder communication.

Each member of the team will take it in turns to dribble the ball through the cones while being both filmed and timed by their teammates. Each performance will be analysed by the team and used to make decisions about what makes a good/poor performance and what changes need to be made to improve. Pupils should have access to paper and pens as well as a range of templates that could support them in recording their findings.

Search for meaning

This task encourages pupils' physical understanding as well as supporting their mathematical and communication skills. However, as pupils are now in mixed-ability groups and working independently of the teacher, they will need differentiated success criteria to ensure that they succeed in all three areas – communication, mathematics and PE. The following criteria should be made available to each group so that they are able to measure their success. The following criteria are an adaptation of the PE Manglish mat for this activity (see pages 130–135).

SUCCESS IN COMMUNICATION, MATHEMATICS AND PE

Blue Gold pupils:

Mathematics:

Calculate potential outcomes.

Calculate the accuracy of their decisions.

Consider different approaches to the problem based on their results.

Communication:

Have extended discussions.

Question each other and build upon what is being said.

Be aware of the effect of their language. A coach needs to be encouraging and may use a different tone of voice to a manager.

Use new subject-specific vocabulary when talking to one another as well as making other effective word choices based on the situation.

PE:

Analyse and comment on skills, techniques and ideas.

Modify and refine their own skills.

Blue Silver pupils:

Mathematics:

Explain their reasoning when making new decisions.

Create their own solutions independently.

Record their findings accurately and explain what they have found out.

Communication:

Are able to listen to ideas and build on them with their own thoughts.

Are aware of the effect of how they choose to communicate (e.g. shouting can have a negative effect but being too quiet can also damage the message).

Use new subject-specific vocabulary when talking to one another and try to find out new words.

PE:

Use their own and others' performances to improve.

Apply skills, techniques and ideas precisely.

Blue Bronze pupils:

Mathematics:

Solve problems practically.

Look for patterns in their findings.

Record their findings accurately.

Communication:

Make eye contact when discussing ideas.

Know how gestures, such as hand signals and confident stature, can have an effect on a listener.

Ask questions about what they have just heard to demonstrate listening skills.

Use full sentences when responding to or explaining an idea.

PE:

Can compare themselves to others.

Select and use skills, actions and ideas appropriately.

Thanks again to collaborative planning, the mathematics teachers have covered data analysis prior to this PE lesson. The pupils are asked to bring along their results to their next maths lesson so that the teacher can review their findings with them. Mathematics and physical education are no longer standalone subjects, sipping tea in their own separate staffrooms, but are now collaborating to create a more joined-up approach to the development of these pupils. Pupils are observing the benefits of mathematical application in a practical subject. This should be happening across the curriculum.

During the activity, pupils are taking it in turns to dribble the ball, film the dribbling and time the run. They are then all working together to analyse the results using the various recording templates (e.g. graphs, bar charts, tally charts). They discuss the results they have recorded and make predictions about what might help them improve. This is why having a stronger member of the team is important as a model for good practice.

To further encourage links between English skills and PE, and to give pupils the opportunity to find words to articulate their new understanding, a word wall presentation (see next page) is made available to them at all times.

The top box is the home slide from a PowerPoint presentation and contains hyperlinks to subject-specific vocabulary and definitions to help pupils better understand what each word means. Some of the simpler words, such as 'movement', lead to synonyms and antonyms as well as explanations, which

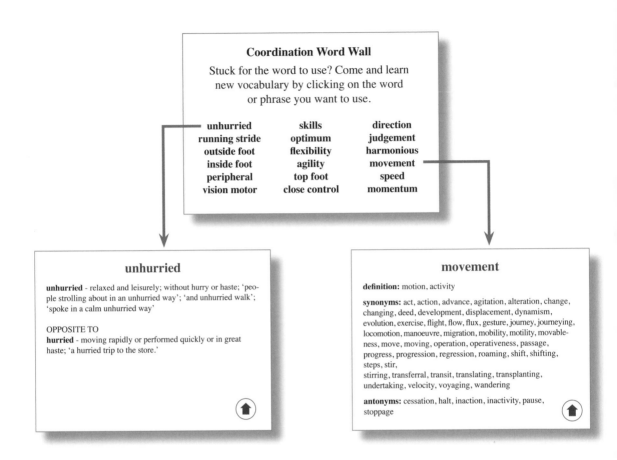

Coordination Word Wall

Stuck for the word to use? Come and learn new vocabulary by clicking on the word or phrase you want to use.

unhurried	skills	direction
running stride	optimum	judgement
outside foot	flexibility	harmonious
inside foot	agility	movement
peripheral	top foot	speed
vision motor	close control	momentum

unhurried

unhurried - relaxed and leisurely; without hurry or haste; 'people strolling about in an unhurried way'; 'and unhurried walk'; 'spoke in a calm unhurried way'

OPPOSITE TO
hurried - moving rapidly or performed quickly or in great haste; 'a hurried trip to the store.'

movement

definition: motion, activity

synonyms: act, action, advance, agitation, alteration, change, changing, deed, development, displacement, dynamism, evolution, exercise, flight, flow, flux, gesture, journey, journeying, locomotion, manoeuvre, migration, mobility, motility, movableness, move, moving, operation, operativeness, passage, progress, progression, regression, roaming, shift, shifting, steps, stir, stirring, transferral, transit, translating, transplanting, undertaking, velocity, voyaging, wandering

antonyms: cessation, halt, inaction, inactivity, pause, stoppage

allows pupils to make more varied vocabulary choices when describing their findings. Each subsequent slide has a home screen button to allow pupils to quickly return to the original slide without coming out of the slideshow or scrolling through all of the information.

This resource could be uploaded onto their laptops or onto a central computer, linked to an interactive whiteboard. Pupils can see from their success criteria (see above) that new subject-specific vocabulary should be used. As they are finding the words to fit their new ideas, they are taking ownership over this new vocabulary. For example, one pupil notices that the ball is going too slowly when another pupil is tapping it softly. They say: 'The ball is going slowly because you're not kicking it hard enough.' The teacher overhears this and asks the pupil if there is a better word to describe what is happening to the ball. The pupil goes to the word wall and eliminates the obvious words such as 'inside foot' and 'outside foot' and reads through some of the other options. He comes back and explains to the other pupil that the ball needs more 'momentum', which can be created by kicking it harder. By making this small change, this pupil has moved from just using appropriate sentences to using subject-specific vocabulary.

By building simple practices like this into lessons, pupils' confidence and fluency with their language will slowly but surely increase. Imagine if this same pupil received this level of communication training in all areas of the curriculum. The Manglish mat is a planning tool designed to make the teacher aware of reading, writing, communication and mathematics during planning. Continued use of this resource during planning should result in teachers of all disciplines recognising such opportunities and acting upon them as they arise.

As the teacher circulates the groups, they are able to use the Manglish criteria to assess pupils' efforts and encourage them to improve. For example, one pupil is observed looking down at their notes and mumbling that they have an idea. The other teammates are not listening and are more concerned with restarting the recording equipment to have another go at observing. This would not be a practical use of their time if one of their members has already solved part of the problem by finding a pattern in their observations.

The teacher is able to ask the group if they have noticed that their team member has an idea – the group were not being rude, they simply had not noticed. The teacher then asks the team member with the idea how they might communicate their idea more fluently. The team member is able to look at the success criteria and notice that if they made eye contact and were more confident in their approach to the team, they would be more likely to command their team's attention. Pupils are being coached in their communication skills which, in turn, will lead to more successful results in their problem-solving and understanding of physical education.

At the end of the activity, pupils must be allowed time to individually gather their results together and make a decision about how they might improve their coordination. **Blue Gold** pupils might have been able to use observations of their teammates to consider many different approaches to the problem. **Blue Silver** pupils may have recorded their findings and been able to discuss the potential in these findings for a solution. **Blue Bronze** pupils may have been able to find a practical solution to the problem by thinking about what makes a good performance. By using the simple gold, silver, bronze steps, the teacher could hand out bronze, silver, gold stickers (or equivalent) to help the pupils recognise their starting points for subsequent lessons.

Demonstrate and teacher review

Having practised their communication skills within their team, pupils are now ready to demonstrate what they have learned about improving coordination using their understanding of effective communication. Each pupil is paired up with a partner from a different group to demonstrate how their problem-solving skills have led them to a solution. It would be a good idea to organise ability pairings before the lesson to allow pupils at a similar level to share appropriate findings. If a pupil working at a far higher level were to demonstrate to a pupil still gaining in confidence at this point, any confidence gained may be diminished.

Pupils teach each other the new ideas they have created to improve their coordination. This exercise will assist in embedding their knowledge of coordination as well as allowing them to gather even more great ideas from each other. The teacher should use this opportunity to look for misconceptions, assess understanding and make decisions about the next direction for their learning.

Home learning

While creating a Manglish curriculum is about avoiding missed opportunities for cross-curricular thinking, trying to cram in activities which have no relevance to the learning of the pupils in that subject is to be avoided at all costs. There were no obvious opportunities to embed good quality writing skills within this lesson. You could argue that during the results analysis, pupils' written skills could have been monitored for accuracy. If this opportunity arose then it should not be passed up, but I felt that communication and mathematics were the key drivers to this lesson.

That said, the opportunity for writing to review is an obvious choice for home learning. Writing to review using the GAP SPLITT planning structure would have been taught to pupils during English lessons. In this instance, their homework would be to review their learning in PE. The English teacher could assess for written skill before passing the homework over to the PE teacher to be reviewed for content.

The following tables are the red and blue Manglish mats used by PE teachers to plan and differentiate over this half-term.

Red Manglish Mat: PE

	Reading	Writing
GOLD	Pupils have an ability to develop a clear critical stance on any text presented to them. They use texts to develop coherent interpretations. Pupils are able to make imaginative, insightful evaluations as a result of their wealth of knowledge of text types, purposes, audiences, language, structure and techniques. Pupils' insights are always well supported by precise reference and wider textual knowledge. Pupils fully appreciate the overall effect of texts of various different genres. They show clear understanding and critical evaluation of writers' purposes and viewpoints and how these are articulated throughout the text. Pupils are independently critical of texts and their origins. They analyse and evaluate texts to determine for themselves how texts relate to particular contexts and traditions and how they may be received over time.	Sentence structures are used imaginatively and with precision to have specific effects throughout the text. Structural devices, language and techniques manipulate readers depending upon the purpose of the text. Pupils have an original style and, thanks to a wide-ranging knowledge of text types and purposes, can manipulate different genres successfully. A range of viewpoints can be skilfully adopted with ease. Correct spelling and effective, imaginatively chosen, ambitious vocabulary is used throughout.

Communication	Term-specific mathematics	Using and applying mathematics
Pupils demonstrate that they can make creative selections from a wide repertoire of strategies and conventions to meet varied speaking and listening challenges.	Pupils can:	Pupils confidently use their knowledge of mathematics to develop their own alternative methods and approaches to creating solutions.
Pupils consciously adapt their vocabulary, grammar and non-verbal features to any situation, including group-working roles, speeches, debates and drama.	Estimate and find the median, quartiles and interquartile range for large data sets, including using a cumulative frequency diagram.	Pupils select and combine known facts and problem-solving strategies to solve problems of increasing complexity.
Pupils are able to sustain concentrated and sensitive listening; they respond with flexibility to creatively develop the ideas of others.	Compare two or more distributions and make inferences, using the shape of the distributions and measures of average and spread, including median and quartiles.	Pupils confidently convey mathematical meaning through precise and consistent use of symbols.
Pupils can exploit a range of dramatic approaches and techniques creatively to create complex and believable roles.	Know when to add or multiply two probabilities.	Pupils take nothing at face value and always further examine generalisations or solutions.
Pupils have an excellent knowledge of spoken language features and continually reflect on their own and others' choices.	Use tree diagrams to calculate probabilities of combinations of independent events.	Pupils are able to comment constructively on the reasoning and logic of processes employed, with the ability to suggest alternative approaches which may produce more accurate results.

Red Manglish mat: PE

	Reading	Writing
SILVER	Pupils are developing an ability to choose their evidence precisely to support their arguments or conclusions.	Pupils effectively use a variety of sentence types and punctuation to achieve purpose and overall effect.
	Pupils' ability to draw on knowledge of other sources to develop or clinch an argument is clearly developing as they have their own insights into texts after teasing out meanings and weighing up evidence. For example, they may reject an argument after exploring what is left unsaid and after comparing it to the rest of the evidence gathered.	Pupils plan the organisation of the text with the purpose in mind. Paragraphs may flow effortlessly into each other or sections may stand out for increased clarity. Openings may be linked with endings to create the echo of an argument.
	Pupils show an appreciation for a writer's use of language, structure and techniques and use their understanding of this to analyse texts for their purpose and effect.	Pupils create a range of texts with distinct and original viewpoints (not necessarily their own). When pupils are making vocabulary or technique choices, they think creatively about the effect on their purpose and audience.
		Pupils use correct spelling throughout and challenge themselves with their vocabulary choices.

Communication	Term-specific mathematics	Using and applying mathematics
Pupils are capable of using speech to explore a wide range of subjects. Planned talks are delivered to create specific effects upon different audiences. Pupils' choices of vocabulary, grammar and non-verbal features are apt and effective. Pupils can adapt easily to new audiences and purposes including a variety of group-working roles. When listening to others, pupils are able to interrogate and extend upon what is said with well-judged questions delivered in a way which extends the speaker's thinking. When creating roles, pupils make insightful choices of speech, gesture, movement and dramatic approaches with confidence. Pupils' knowledge of spoken language allows them to evaluate the meaning and impact of how they and others use and adapt language for specific purposes.	Pupils can: Suggest a problem to explore using statistical methods, frame questions and raise conjectures, and identify possible sources of bias and plan how to minimise it. Select, construct and modify (on paper and using ICT) suitable graphical representation to progress an enquiry, including frequency polygons and lines of best fit on scatter graphs. Estimate the mean, median and range of a set of grouped data and determine the modal class, selecting the statistic most appropriate to the line of enquiry. Compare two or more distributions and make inferences, using the shape of the distributions and measures of average and range. Understand relative frequency as an estimate of probability and use this to compare outcomes of an experiment, examine critically the results of a statistical enquiry and justify the choice of statistical representation in written presentation.	Pupils are able to use their mathematically reasoned research to evaluate future solutions. Pupils' confidence in the application of mathematics allows them to explore connections in mathematics across a range of contexts. Pupils appreciate the difference between a mathematical argument and experimental evidence. They are able to use and present both using a wealth of presentational structures. Pupils confidently justify their findings and create effective solutions based on accurately reasoned mathematical evidence.

Red Manglish mat: PE

	Reading	Writing
BRONZE	When using texts as evidence, pupils make relevant points, including summary and synthesis of information from different sources or different places in the same text. Pupils' comments are securely based in textual evidence and they explore layers of meaning. Pupils recognise why the writer has structured the work in a specific way to create the overall effect on the reader. Pupils understand how the writer has used language and techniques and can trace them throughout a text to give a detailed explanation of the text as a whole. They begin to consider wider implications, layers of meaning and different audiences over different time periods when discussing this. Pupils use the context of a text to identify the writer's intended purpose and effect. They can easily identify the viewpoint of a text and its role in the purpose and effect. Pupils can discuss in detail how a text is affected by its context. Pupils recognise how the meaning and reception of a text can change over time and how conventions of text types can change over time.	Pupils use a full range of sentence structures and they are beginning to use them to manipulate their readers. Pupils are confident with their use of punctuation and use it to create effects. Before proofreading, pupils may still make errors with ambitious structures but can spot these errors before redrafting. When planning, pupils make choices about the structure of the text to have specific effects on the reader. For example, if they are creating an informative leaflet, they may begin with an image that further explains the writing followed by clear bullet points. Pupils plan to use certain language choices and techniques to create more convincing viewpoints. They are aware of the conventions associated with a range of text types and use this information to make their text convincing. Pupils use correct spelling throughout, including some ambitious, uncommon words. Pupils actively seek to increase their vocabulary.

Communication	Term-specific mathematics	Using and applying mathematics
Pupils can explore complex ideas in a range of ways. They are able to keep talk succinct or extend upon points for greater clarity.	Pupils can:	Pupils show confidence when identifying and solving mathematical problems.
Pupils are controlled in their planned talks and guide listeners as a result of their structure. Pupils adapt vocabulary, grammar and non-verbal features depending upon the situation.	Design a survey or experiment to capture the necessary data from one or more sources. Design, trial and, if necessary, refine data collection sheets; construct tables for large discrete and continuous sets of raw data, choosing suitable class intervals.	Pupils recognise when it is sensible to order their investigations into smaller, more manageable tasks. When presenting their findings, pupils interpret, discuss and synthesise information in a variety of mathematical forms. Their argument is effectively reasoned using symbols, diagrams and graphs, and related explanatory texts use logical argument to establish the truth of a statement.
Pupils can engage with complex discussion, adapting to any group role and listening to a range of points before making perceptive responses. They show an awareness of the speaker's aims and extended meanings but question them further adding more to the discussion.	Design and use two-way tables. They are able to select, construct and modify (on paper and using ICT) pie charts, bar charts, frequency diagrams, simple time graphs and scatter graphs. They will be able to identify which of the above is most useful depending on the problem being tackled.	
Pupils are flexible in their choices of speech, gesture and movement, and can create different roles convincingly.	Find and record all possible mutually exclusive outcomes for single events and two successive events in a systematic way.	
Pupils have a wide-ranging knowledge of spoken language features and use them to recognise spoken language choices made by others.	Know that the sum of probabilities of all mutually exclusive outcomes is 1 and use this when solving problems, and communicate interpretations and results of a statistical survey using selected tables, graphs and diagrams in support.	

Blue Manglish Mat: PE

	Reading	Writing
GOLD	Pupils are selective about their use of evidence and can use quotations to back up their deductions about the text. Pupils infer meaning and deduce using examples from the text to back up their ideas. Pupils are able to identify how the text is organised and can refer to a range of features (e.g. 'Images are used to demonstrate where muscles are in the body'). Pupils are able to identify a range of language features used by the writer with some explanation (e.g. 'When it gets to the climax they speak in short sentences and quickly which makes it more tense'). Pupils can easily identify the viewpoint of a text (e.g. 'The writer is strongly against the use of anabolic steroids'). Pupils can confidently identify text types for different purposes, such as leaflets, articles and instruction manuals. When identifying the main purpose of a text, pupils are able to comment on how the context of a text can affect the meaning. For example, an instruction manual provided by the manufacturer is likely to be more accurate than Wikipedia.	Pupils use a full range of sentence structures for different purposes. Pupils can use a full range of punctuation correctly. They may make mistakes when attempting ambitious structures (e.g. 'The ball was, during the first half of the match at least, in my control, I used my right foot to pass between players.' Here the first use of commas for parenthesis is correct, but the second should be a semicolon as both sides of the comma could stand alone as sentences). Pupils plan their paragraphs to create a coherent and logical structure. Their openings and endings are effective. Connectives are used throughout to signal changes in time or message (e.g. therefore, however, unlike, before, meanwhile). Pupils plan their viewpoint and make vocabulary choices with the purpose and audience in mind. They are convincing. Pupils spell all common words correctly and no longer make mistakes with homophones. Pupils use dictionaries effectively to find new spellings. More complicated spellings may be incorrect (e.g. outrageous, exaggerated, announcing, parallel). Pupils should be provided with challenging topic-specific vocabulary lists.

Communication	Term-specific mathematics	Using and applying mathematics
Pupils elaborate upon points to express and explain relevant ideas and feelings. Pupils plan what they say to make their meaning clear and to have an effect upon, as well as to engage, the listener. Pupils deliberately match vocabulary, grammar and non-verbal features to their audience, purpose and context. When listening to others, pupils recognise implicit meanings and develop upon what has been said with comments and questions. Pupils are able to take on a range of roles in groups effectively and are able to take a leading role in shaping discussions, as well as developing characters beyond themselves through deliberate choices of speech, movement and gesture. Pupils are able to explain features of their own and others' language use, showing understanding of effect of varying language for different purposes and situations.	Pupils can: Ask questions, plan how to answer them and collect the data required in terms of probability. Select methods based on equally likely outcomes and experimental evidence, as appropriate. Understand and use the probability scale from 0 to 1. Understand and use the mean of discrete data and compare two simple distributions, using the range and one of mode, median or mean. Understand that different outcomes may result from repeating an experiment, interpret graphs and diagrams, (including pie charts) and draw conclusions, and create and interpret line graphs where the intermediate values have meaning.	Pupils independently identify mathematical problems and are able to obtain the necessary information to come up with solutions. For example, pupils may choose to compare the effect of using their left foot to their right by making a tally of mistakes made during a game using each. Pupils independently check results, considering whether these are reasonable. Pupils apply their new learning from mathematics lessons to new investigations from a range of contexts. Pupils are confident when speaking using newly acquired mathematical language and interpreting symbols and diagrams to explain their own logical reasoning of problems.

Blue Manglish Mat: PE

	Reading	Writing
SILVER	When using the text to support their ideas, pupils can refer to points in the text to back up their ideas but often paraphrase rather than make clear selections. When inferring meaning, pupils are able to refer to points in the text to explain why they think their ideas about it are correct. Pupils are able to recognise why a text has been ordered in the way it has. For example, the writer uses bullet points to highlight their main points or a real-life example first to set the scene. Pupils are able to pick out word classes and techniques, such as verbs or alliteration, and explain why the writer has chosen them. For example, they may say that a writer has chosen to use the personal pronouns 'you' and 'we' to include the reader in the explanation. Pupils can comment on the intended effect of a text on a reader (e.g. 'The text is written to inform readers of the correct way to warm up. It is likely the text was created to avoid injury'). Pupils can recognise features common to different text types. For example, pupils will recognise the presentational features of a newspaper report and know that a leaflet is presented differently. When identifying the main purpose of a text, pupils understand that writers have their own opinions and that it is important to know where a text is set and who wrote it.	Pupils are beginning to use complex sentences, as well as simple and compound sentences, and they are learning to use subordinate clauses (e.g. 'After dribbling the ball past the second cone, I found it was easier to use my right foot than my left'). Pupils write in the correct tense with occasional errors. Pupils can use full stops, capital letters, question marks, exclamation marks and speech marks without making mistakes. Pupils can use commas in lists and are learning to use them to indicate subordinate clauses. Pupils plan topics for each of their paragraphs and begin each paragraph with a topic sentence. Ideas are in a logical order. Sentences are connected with more varied connectives, such as 'also' or 'then', but one or more can often be overused. Pupils can create a believable viewpoint and match it to their purpose and readers, although they are not always consistent. They elaborate on ideas by using expanded noun and adverbial phrases (e.g. 'Quickly, I kicked the football hard and fast'). Pupils choose their vocabulary deliberately to match their purpose but are not overly ambitious with their choices. Pupils' spelling of common words is correct. This includes spelling rules for suffixes such as adding -ly and changing tense. Homophones may still be confused. Provide pupils with a unit-specific word bank to support spelling of new vocabulary.

Communication	Term-specific mathematics	Using and applying mathematics
Pupils are able to speak in extended turns to express their ideas and feelings. They have given thought to how their listener may respond before they speak. As a listener, they consider what has been said and comment upon it showing understanding. Pupils recognise that vocabulary, grammar and non-verbal features should be adapted, depending on the purpose and audience of their speaking. Pupils understand the purpose of different roles in groups and show that they have attempted to adapt their talk to suit the needs of their situation. Pupils are able to create different roles and begin to make deliberate choices of speech, gesture, language and movement.	Pupils can: Collect and record discrete group data. Continue to use Venn and Carroll diagrams to record their sorting and classifying of information. Construct and interpret frequency diagrams and simple line graphs. Understand and use the mode and range to describe sets of data.	Pupils are able to develop their own strategies for solving simple problems. Pupils can apply newly acquired mathematics to practical contexts. For example, they have just learned to sort and classify information and so may decide to sort physical techniques into separate tests before collating their evidence later. Pupils always present information and results in a clear and organised way.

Blue Manglish Mat: PE

	Reading	Writing
BRONZE	Pupils can read a text fluently and use their understanding of phonetics to read unfamiliar words out loud. They can work out the meanings of new words. Pupils can recognise and retell the main points of the text. Pupils can use the text as an example but will often retell the story of the text rather than using it to support their own ideas. Pupils can recognise word classes, such as adjectives, verbs, nouns and pronouns, within a text but do not comment on why they are used. Pupils can recognise why a writer has written the text (e.g. 'This text is an information leaflet'). Pupils can recognise differences and similarities between texts and their writers' viewpoints by inferring simple meanings. Pupils understand that some newspaper articles may be biased.	Pupils' sentences are often basic. For example, using only simple sentences ('Taking part in sport keeps you healthy') or compound sentences ('Taking part in sport keeps you healthy and doing a sport you like is best'). Pupils will most commonly use 'and', 'but' and 'so' to connect sentences. Pupils do not always use the right tense for their writing and may even switch between tenses without any purpose. Pupils can use capital letters, full stops, exclamation marks and question marks in the right places. Pupils will order their text logically but may not use clear paragraphs. Links are made between ideas in the writing but some ideas may appear disjointed. Pupils can adopt a viewpoint. For example, if they are asked to create a leaflet against the use of steroids in sport they can use negative vocabulary to express this view. Pupils may need support with setting out their work to match the style of the genre. Pupils use words that are appropriate to the set task but are not ambitious in their vocabulary choices. Common words are spelled correctly and unfamiliar words are often written phonetically. Pupils may need support with spelling and should be given unit-specific word banks. Homophones are likely to cause confusion (e.g. there, their, they're; too, two, to).

Communication	Term-specific mathematics	Using and applying mathematics
Pupils can present how they feel to one another by taking turns in extended speaking about a topic, while maintaining eye contact and using gesticulation to further express their feelings.	Pupils can:	Pupils are able to select the mathematics they want to use, from a range provided by the teacher, to solve mathematical problems. They may choose to use a tally chart to record the number of mistakes made in a test.
	Gather information.	
	Construct bar charts and pictograms, where the symbol represents a group of units.	
Pupils show that they are listening to other speakers' main ideas by making comments and suggestions.	Use Venn and Carroll diagrams to record their sorting and classifying of information.	Pupils try out different simple mathematical approaches to find ways of overcoming problems.
Pupils try out different roles in groups and attempt to take on different viewpoints or roles by adapting what they say and how they say it.	Extract and interpret information presented in simple tables, lists, bar charts and pictograms.	Pupils begin to organise their work logically and check their results are accurate. Pupils may use a calculator to check that survey results have been added up correctly.
		Pupils are able to use and interpret mathematical symbols and diagrams. For example, pupils may use graphs representing the effect of trying out different techniques.

3 Project X

Why run Project X?

Everyone involved in the Manglish curriculum (not just the pupils) has just spent the last five terms working hard, learning about the importance of cross-curricular knowledge and the practical application of reading, writing, communication and mathematics skills in every subject. In a perfect scenario, Manglish pupils are now easily able to form links between seemingly unrelated concepts to create new ideas, and can apply knowledge and skills from across the curriculum purposefully. Teachers are now confident and skilled in developing opportunities to embed reading, writing, communication and mathematics skills and they have taught everything that is set out in government guidelines, leaving the final half-term to use all of that valuable learning in a very special project.

This half-term is a time for teachers to enjoy the spoils of their hard work and for the school to think big. The big idea for this half-term is called Project X because one size will never fit all. Every year this project runs, it will never look the same twice. It will become whatever you make it. The X stands for each new, treasured experience that will develop through application, collaboration and creativity. Pupils will be given the opportunity to apply all that they have learned in a practical, real-life project which allows them to come into their own; teachers will bask in the glory of their creations as they watch their students succeed.

Doing something different, something creative and something that is real will show pupils (and teachers) how all learning is applicable beyond school, and that all subjects can be used purposefully when working on a big project together. In their first year of Manglish, teachers will have worked hard! Changing the way that you work isn't easy, but it is worth it. Project X is a time to enjoy the results of that hard work as pupils put into practice what they have learned, facilitated by their teachers. During this half-term, pupils are not being examined on individual subjects, but on their ability to practically apply their learning in an authentic context. This half-term will result in the achievement of something great, something that we can be proud of and that pupils can build upon for the rest of their lives.

How do I get it right?

The project does not need to have a specific formula, as long as it explicitly allows pupils to practice their reading, writing, communication and mathematical skills in a purposeful and engaging way. The project should demonstrate to pupils the positive and creative effects of joined-up thinking and collaboration. Therefore, the borders between subjects should be taken down and replaced with effective and obvious links.

Pupils will benefit, as will teachers, if everyone is working towards a common goal. So what are you going to do? How brave are you feeling? As we have planned to cover all of the government-dictated content by the end of half-term 5, this half-term is about the deliberate practice of skills and knowledge. We can begin to get seriously inventive with our curriculum. Would you dare reorganise the whole half-term so that teachers from across the school team teach a combination of subjects? Would you be less brave and collapse the timetable for a week to undergo collaborative projects? Or would one day in this half-term be enough for you? The end product is up to you.

Example Project X

Local community festival

This festival is to be designed, advertised and professionally executed by all Year 7 pupils. The pupils are to create a festival which is both entertaining and educational, and has the potential to attract visitors from far and wide. During the previous half-term (or even earlier, depending on how much time may be required to plan the bigger picture of your project) teachers have collaboratively agreed on the project and how their subject will contribute to its success. In this example, teachers have decided that they want pupils to really get to know their local area and to give something back to their community. They plan to run a festival with the end goal of raising awareness about a campaign to regenerate a local area (to be designed by one group of pupils – see the table below). Everyone works together to make the day a success and a big pile of fun!

During the early stages of planning, teachers have grouped themselves into specialist areas to make up the necessary teams to run the festival smoothly. Teachers have chosen areas they enjoy because Project X is not only about pupils coming into their own, but about teachers being excited to come into work every day and make this happen. For this reason, each teacher should be involved in a specialist area that really appeals to them. Pupils flourish when they enter the real world beyond school in a field that interests them. However, we don't ordinarily allow eleven- and twelve-year-olds to specialise as we feel they are still too young to recognise which avenue is right for them and they still have much to learn. This project gives pupils a chance to practise becoming a specialist for a short time, while also demonstrating the importance of all other subjects in contributing to the success of their specialism. They should enter their next year of school with a reinvigorated sense of the purposefulness of every subject's role in the creation of them as a citizen ready to embrace any new learning experience that comes their way post school.

Prior to this half-term, teachers advertise their specialisms and students sign up for the area that they feel best suits them. There is a limit to the number of pupils per team to ensure that groups are manageable, so pupils should sign up to options in their order of preference. The teachers running the individual areas of the project will have the final say on who joins their team. Each team has a maths and English specialist assigned to them as a project coordinator because reading, writing, communication and mathematics skills are the driving force behind the success of the project.

The following table is an example of how teachers might advertise potential projects for the festival to their pupils to encourage them to sign up:

Regeneration project Teachers involved: Geography and citizenship English and maths	We are looking for a team of 30 innovative pupils to take part in a regeneration proposal. We will investigate our locality for areas which are poorly used and develop a plan of action to have them regenerated with the needs of the community in mind. As part of the festival, we will create a stand that promotes our plan to the local council, residents and businesses, with the view to having our plan put into practice.
Entertainment team Teachers involved: Music and history English and maths	We are looking for a team of 30 pupils to join our entertainment team. This team will provide the musical and dramatic entertainment for the event. Visitors will be able to enjoy the background music as they enjoy the festivities and also will be educated in the origins of music from the local area. We are looking for musicians to join our band and budding actors, actresses, scriptwriters and directors to help us develop a play about the local community which visitors can enjoy for a small donation towards the regeneration project.
Promotions and advertising Teachers involved: MFL and computing English and maths	We are recruiting a team of 30 pupils to be part of our promotional team. You will be responsible for developing advertising materials, including leaflets, newspaper articles, a website and logos. Effective communication skills are essential as you will be responsible for communicating with all other teams to ensure that their events are properly promoted. As we are twinned with a school in Spain, it is essential that all of our promotional materials are accurately translated into Spanish.

Wildlife investigations Teachers involved: Science and geography English and maths	We are looking for a team of no more than 20 investigators to scientifically analyse the wildlife in the surrounding areas. We will produce a professional field guide to be sold during the festival to raise funds for the regeneration project. We will also have a visitor's stand where people can learn about the issues our local wildlife faces as a result of current industry practices in the area. We want to investigate what those issues are and develop possible solutions to the problems.
Business links Teachers involved: Technology and citizenship English and maths	We are looking to employ 30 pupils to make links with our local industries. Our aim is to engage local businesses to take part in our festival and run workshops to educate people about their profession and how their work contributes to the community. The role will involve actively taking part in the development and execution of the workshops. Workshops could include baking, fishing, car manufacturing, customer service, etc. It will be up to you to source the business links and support in the development of an engaging and informative workshop to be enjoyed by visitors.
The gallery Teachers involved: History and art English and maths	We are looking for 20 budding artists to produce an art display for the festival. We will be creating one-off pieces that represent our local culture and its historical significance. The artwork will be displayed throughout the day and auctioned online at the end of the festival to raise money towards the regeneration project.
Fit and fun Teachers involved: PE and science English and maths	We are looking for 30 active pupils to run a series of traditional sporting events on the day of the festival. We will be teaming up with local fitness providers to provide a comprehensive guide to the science behind keeping fit and where to do it in our local area. We will be producing a professional guide which will be sold from our stand at the festival, the proceeds of which will contribute towards the regeneration project.

Catering team Teachers involved: Technology and science English and maths	We are recruiting 30 pupils to our festival catering team. This team will be providing traditional recipes using locally sourced ingredients. Our stand will educate visitors about how to create traditional healthy meals on a budget. We will also be selling a professional recipe book. The proceeds from the food sold and the book will all go towards the regeneration project.
Coordinators and managers Teachers involved: English and maths	We are recruiting 16 pupils (2 from each of the above teams) as project coordinators and 2 pupils to be project managers. Coordinators will be responsible for the effective communication between teams and budgeting within your individual team. You will be expected to attend all planning meetings and feed back information to your group. Managers will be responsible for the effective organisation of the event as a whole. We want to create an exciting, entertaining and educational event that attracts visitors from afar and supports the local area.

Pupils will continue to attend individual subject lessons and be taught about their local community from a variety of angles:

Art	**Exploration of local artists both present day and historical** Visiting local galleries and being inspired by emerging local art movements and artists.
Citizenship	**The issues and needs of our local area** What problems are we facing as a community? What problems can we solve as a school? Homelessness? Unemployment? Lack of support for elderly citizens? Racial divides? Lack of recreational areas?
Computing	**Local business to international conglomerate** The Internet and its infinite possibilities for the growth of a small idea.
English	Reading skills involved in investigating the needs of the festival. Writing skills required to create programmes, information, promotional materials and articles. Communication skills involved in a large group project, dealing with local businesses, giving professional educational talks, confidence, etc.
Geography	**The make-up of our local area** Population, industries, attractions, immigration, tourism, where we sit in the country, where we sit in the world.
History	**Our local area through the ages** How did our community evolve to where we are in the present day?
Maths	Mathematical skills involved in the creation of an event, such as budgeting, timings, effective use of space, numbers for safety, etc.
MFL	**Tourism and promotion to reach a wider audience** The MFL department will twin with a school in Spain and create a website to translate the festival information into Spanish for pupils in their twinned school to enjoy. Pupils from the school could also be invited over for the event.
Music	**Composition of music for a varied audience** The festival will have many visitors with varying musical tastes and this should be considered during the composition of the entertainment. For the festival, pupils will be performing through drama, music and song.

PE	**Healthy living and our local area** How can we take PE beyond the classroom? Looking at sporting venues, clubs, classes, etc.
Science	**Our local area and evolution** Awareness of the biology all around us.
Technology	**Local industry** What are the industries that keep our community alive (food, agriculture, manufacturing, etc.)? What are the implications for the success of our local industries on our future?

It will be necessary to be creative with the timetable in order to allow pupils time to properly prepare for their individual roles in the project. As maths and English are being supported by every area of the curriculum, it makes sense to take some of their allocated periods to allow a new Project X lesson to appear on the timetable. A typical timetable may look like this:

	Mon	Tues	Wed	Thur	Fri
Period 1	English	Geography	History	Maths	Geography
Period 2	MFL	English	Maths	History	Science
Period 3	Science	Computing	Project X	Project X	Art
Period 4	Technology	PE	Project X	Project X	Music
Period 5	Technology	PE	Project X	Project X	Citizenship

During the first few weeks, Project X lessons will require sessions for investigation and research, followed by time for creation, critique and perfection, and ending with final preparations for the event. The objective is for pupils to become experts in their chosen specialist area. As all curriculum areas are working towards a common goal, pupils will be drawing on knowledge from all areas of the curriculum in their creations, especially the underpinning skills of reading, writing, communication and mathematics (RWCM). Teachers use their knowledge of these four skills to identify the opportunities that already exist in this realistic setting, as set out on the table on the following page:

Regeneration project Geography and citizenship English and maths	R Investigation into example regeneration projects.	W Planning the persuasive and professional pitch for the regeneration project. Writing a proposal for the council.
Entertainment team Music and history English and maths	R Investigations into the history of music in the local area.	W Composing songs. Writing a play.
Promotions and advertising MFL and computing English and maths	R Interpreting the needs of all groups. Reading examples of effective advertising campaigns.	W Planning and creating promotional materials, including viral advertisements, apps, leaflets, newspaper articles and posters. Pupils will use email as a form of written communication with other groups.
Wildlife investigations Science and geography English and maths	R Pupils will research articles detailing what is already written about the local area in preparation for their fresh investigation.	W Pupils must plan and execute professional, informative writing.
Business links Technology and citizenship English and maths	R Investigation of local businesses and their origins. Pupils must decide on the most effective businesses to run informative workshops on the day. Poor choices could result in a poor show.	W Pupils must plan and write up their workshops in conjunction with their chosen employers. Writing of promotional material is ultimately down to the promotions team but explaining the workshop correctly to allow the promotions team to do their job will be done via email.

C Communicating with locals to explore their needs. Working as a team towards a final successful outcome.	**M** Working out the costs of the regeneration project. How can they develop an area that has been long forgotten and generate income for the community?
C Dramatic performances and confidence in delivery. Pupils will also communicate appropriately when educating the visitors on the day.	**M** Pupils will be given a production budget and should develop a strategy for keeping overheads low and making money on the day.
C All groups are being represented through this team and so effective listening and communication is a must.	**M** Space and shape will be practised through the creation of promotional materials. Pupils will also be responsible for budgeting.
C Pupils will be running an informative stall and must be able to effectively and appropriately communicate with visitors.	**M** Estimations based on their investigation and probabilities of events in the future. Use of graphs and charts to support their informative writing. Pupils will need to keep overheads low in order to make a profit on the field guide.
C Pupils must sensitively and effectively work with local business owners, encouraging them to take part. Pupils must communicate with visitors on the day to run effective and informative workshops.	**M** Pupils should learn about the local economy as they investigate the effect of local businesses on their community. They must also manage the budget for their workshops.

The gallery History and art English and maths	R Investigations into local artists and art movements.	W Pupils will write an explanatory description of their artwork to be displayed by the piece for the enjoyment of visitors.
Fit and fun PE and science English and maths	R Pupils will investigate traditional pursuits while preparing the activities for the day. They will also investigate the local area for fitness clubs. Pupils will research the effects of different exercises and activities on the body in preparation for producing their guide.	W Pupils will plan and create a professional, informative booklet.
Catering team Technology and science English and maths	R Investigation of local produce and traditional recipes.	W Pupils will be writing a recipe book of their own with details about how to source local produce. Pupils will create their own branding and packaging which will be finalised by the promotions team to tie in with the day.
Coordinators and managers English and maths	R Managers and coordinators must be made aware of the activities taking place across all projects so that they can ensure consistency.	W Pupils will be writing the plans for the day and ensuring that all intended outcomes for visitors are met.

The final event will be a spectacular one to be enjoyed by the whole community. People will be educated by the pupils about their home town and its industry, history, cuisine and potential. Everyone involved will accomplish something big, successful and, best of all, something real.

C Pupils will communicate with the promotions team to develop an effective auction website to sell the artwork after the event. Pupils will also interact with the visitors on the day to educate them about their work.	M Pupils may employ rules of proportion while creating artistic works. Pupils must keep to a budget for their creations.
C Pupils will be planning in teams and running events on the day of the festival. Pupils must be effective team workers and confident in their delivery.	M Pupils must work out timings for their activities and keep their overheads low so as to make a profit on the booklets.
C Pupils must be clear communicators as they are going to run workshops on the day to inform visitors about how their food is sourced and made.	M Pupils must compare the prices and quality of products when sourcing produce. When cooking, their knowledge of weights and measures will be applied effectively. Pupils will also need to keep overheads low so that a profit may be made on the food products.
C Pupils will be responsible for the effective communication between all project areas. They will attend meetings to hear progress updates and communicate findings to their groups.	M Pupils will need to manage the budget as a whole to ensure that a profit is made on the day. They will develop effective timings for the smooth running of the day. Pupils will create a floor plan to scale to ensure that the event is safe and comfortable for the expected number of visitors.

Case study Project X in a single day

The project outlined above is ambitious. It requires detailed planning and will require the whole school to be on board. If you love the idea but are nervous about taking such a huge step, this case study could provide you with inspiration for a Manglish day on a much smaller scale. Chris Curtis of Saint John Houghton Catholic Voluntary Academy, in Ilkeston, was inspired by the ideas behind Manglish and set up a Project X day in his school called the Mash-Up Day. Here are his reflections:[1]

After attending a conference for 'Outstanding Literacy in Secondary Schools', and thoroughly enjoying it, I was inspired by the presentation Lisa Ashes gave about her concept of a collaborative curriculum nicknamed Manglish. The ideas presented during this talk floated in my brain for several months and, in my role as literacy coordinator, I decided to use them to plan a Manglish day. I thought, what if we did lots of mixes? What if we mash-up subjects for just one day? The Mash-Up Day was born.

This is how I presented it to staff:

What is a mash-up?

The Mash-up Day is about making links between subjects explicit. Our students do not always use the knowledge from one subject to help them with the learning in another. By forcing connections, pupils will see the benefits of making these connections in future.

The objectives were to:

> Develop links across departments.
> Develop students' ability to make connections.
> Provide a real context and audience for a piece of writing.
> Develop teachers' confidence in teaching literacy.

---

1   This has been adapted from Chris's excellent blog post, Mashing-Up Literacy, *Learning from my Mistakes: An English Teacher's Blog* (1 August 2013). Available at: <http://learningfrommymistakesenglish. blogspot.co.uk/2013/08/mashing-up-literacy.html?m-1>.

> Think creatively.

> Get students working collaboratively with others in different year groups.

The teachers were very responsive to the idea. We decided to collapse the timetable for a day and do something different. The basic plan for the day went like this:

Period 1: Subject mash-up

Period 2: Subject mash-up

Period 3: Written reflection on the mash-up

Period 4: Read the booklet made of their reflections

The mash-up lessons took place at the start of the day and helped to generate a piece of writing. The writing could be anything generated from the lesson. However, the writing had a real and genuine audience: the rest of the school. Pupils were writing for their peers – real writing that would be judged by others that very day. This reality added a new aspect to their writing. At the end of the day, we would all read the booklets to examine the outcomes of the mash-ups that we hadn't taken part in.

The build-up to the day was amazing. I made sure I had given staff lots of notice so they were able to prepare with plenty of time to spare. During the preparation, you had staff fighting to work with each other. You heard staffroom conversations of potential mash-ups to be done. People continued chatting about it over several weeks as there was a general buzz in the air with colleagues working together in a way that they never had before, collaborating and enjoying making new links. It helped that I didn't make the connections but instead left staff to arrange the subject combinations for themselves. Furthermore, as the day was planned for the end of the academic year, there was less pressure and people felt that there wasn't a major panic about missing valuable teaching time.

The day started with an assembly. I used a collection of my daughters' handbags to express the purpose of the day as a simple metaphor. With some handy volunteers, I got students to each hold a handbag representing a single subject. I explained how lessons involve learning things (cue a plastic ball representing a singular bit of knowledge shoved into each of the bags) and that students often zipped up the bag as soon as they leave a lesson, leaving the knowledge forgotten and unused. Today, they had to open those handbags, swap information between subjects and see how much more effective learning is when handbags are full of knowledge (or plastic balls) from all the other subjects.

The combinations between subjects included:

Penglish – PE and English
Sciglish – Science and English
Frart – French and art
Tecaths – Technology and maths
Spanology – MFL and technology

Half the fun was making up names! It proved infectious and the students began coming up with their own ideas too.

The day was a melting pot of ideas, collaboration and interesting learning experiences. The groups were organised via vertical tutor groups, meaning that each class contained a mixture of pupils from Year 7, 8, 9 and some 10. Roughly, each class had about thirty-two students in it with two teachers team teaching. New connections were being made between subjects, knowledge, skills, staff and students.

The lessons were all individual but had been planned collaboratively between staff members from various departments. Here is just a flavour of some of the things offered:

> **Food and maths** – making cakes and up-scaling the ingredients.
> **French and technology** – designing chocolates and packaging for a new chocolate brand to be sold in France.
> **Maths and technology** – designing and throwing paper aeroplanes and working out the perfect trajectory for maximum flight.
> **Science and English** – experiments with eggs and writing a crazy experiment.
> **PE and English** – writing radio commentaries for a game they played in the first lesson.

> **French and art** – researching a French artist and developing French skills through art.
> **French and ICT** – designing a French superhero and creating their Wikipedia page.

There were fifteen different mash-ups across the school and, as an initial experiment, it produced some fruitful end results. For me, working with another teacher and implementing English skills in a science lesson was eye-opening and allowed us both to see the obvious connections between our usually insular subjects.

Pupils wrote up their reflections on the mash-ups and this, as well as allowing them to write for their peers, provided me with a booklet full of exemplar writing from the day. Pupils read and critiqued each other's mash-up writing, providing each other with detailed feedback on written skills and further opening up minds to the possibilities of using learning in one subject and actually applying it in the next.

The students loved the day, feeling that it made them see subjects in a different light. Some were so keen that they suggested, next time, we mix three or more subjects at once. As part of the evaluation process, the students got a chance to suggest their own mash-ups. Of course, PE was linked to every subject under the sun, but some interesting combinations were made, such as exploring history through PE by looking at old games from the past and using geography in a cooking lesson to explore different cultures and cuisines.

The problem is that currently literacy has this big fanfare moment and, in some cases, people feel that their subject is being neglected as a result. This mashing up of subjects in the Manglish style highlights the equal nature of all subjects. Running this Manglish day meant that we were raising the status of every subject and showing students that we are working as a team. Literacy runs at the heart of every subject, supporting their outcomes rather than taking their subject over. The mash-up or Manglish day was a resounding success; I am glad we mashed things up. Some of the suggestions Lisa presents sound a little scary and ambitious. I think that starting small with this little experiment worked as the first step. We hope to keep getting bigger, and who knows what we might do next?

Further suggestions for Project X

Project fortnight

A well-known school in Northumberland runs a successful project fortnight every year. This two-week event happens in the final half-term when all Year 11 pupils have left school and all Year 10 pupils are out on work experience. The whole Key Stage 3 cohort are taken off timetable and sign up to a project of their choice. Just like in the example half-term Project X, teachers collaborate across the curriculum and design projects based on their individual passions. Teachers promote their projects to pupils and pupils choose to take part in those that interest them. The groups work together for the whole two weeks and do not take part in any traditional subjects. Instead, they spend time investigating, preparing, critiquing and making their final products. Unlike the Manglish example, teachers' projects are not linked with one another but they do all culminate in a final show where parents and the local community are invited in to view the pupils' efforts.

Music festival

You could run a music festival. Although this seems to favour one subject over the others, think of the possibilities: pupils could create merchandise for the festival, run food and drink stands, create promotional material, develop competitions, produce original music, produce the setting and so on. All subjects could be involved in the creation of the festival and the final product would be the talk of the town!

Historic festival

If you live in a historically significant area, why not run a history festival? Again, one subject is at the forefront but all the other subjects contribute to the success of the final product. You could design historically accurate costumes, create a realistic setting and invite people from far and wide to come and learn from your school.

Pupils as publishers

A completely different approach could be to collaboratively write a book. Now that we are fully immersed in the digital age, you don't need big publishers to produce a book – you just need to write one and decide how best to get it published.[2] The book could be based on anything at all, such as a selection of short stories written by the pupils. A website could be created to promote the book and you could hold a book launch event run by the pupils.

When creating your project, remember:

> Project X should make learning come to life.
> Do something that has real-world implications so that pupils can see the benefits of their learning in reality.
> Keep reading, writing, communication and mathematics skills at the heart of your planning and ensure that those skills are clearly identified during the initial planning stages.
> Think carefully about your own school's circumstances.
> Be inventive with your ideas.

Just think of the rich opportunities to purposefully practise reading, writing, communication and mathematics that will arise from such a venture. With Project X there are infinite possibilities that are only limited by your imagination. Think big and you will get a big result; think a little smaller and you may not have a huge impact but you will still achieve awareness.

---

2   There are numerous online websites dedicated to self-publishing (e.g. www.blurb.co.uk, www.lulu.com, www.booksurge.com) which makes getting published so much easier.

4 Manglish our future

Why do we need Manglish?

The government wants our education system to compete with the best in the world for a very good reason – to avoid economic disaster. The real cost to countries like England, which have a high proportion of pupils leaving secondary education with weak literacy and numeracy skills, can be assessed in monetary terms. For example, according to KPMG, the annual cost to the public purse arising from the failure of young people to master basic numeracy skills is up to £2.4 billion.[1] Thanks to the introduction of the National Literacy Strategy in 1997, literacy has had far more publicity and, as a result, the percentage of illiterate school leavers has decreased. So, it is possible for educators to work together to put a stop to pupils leaving school without the literacy and numeracy skills needed for a fruitful and productive life.

If we are going to produce pupils who can apply their education, as a whole, to real-life contexts, pupils who can develop solutions to our uncertain economic future, pupils who can develop more economically effective ways

---

1   See <http://www.nationalnumeracy.org.uk/resources/14/index.html?term=kpmg>.

of living, then a Manglish curriculum is essential. At the heart of Manglish are the skills that will create the literate and numerate minds that are going to shape the future of our world. Teachers of all subjects are lynchpins in ensuring that the education we provide creates joined-up thinking in the minds of young people.

Education is in the business of manufacturing the brainpower of the future. Not a business in the sense of developing free schools and academies in order to generate more cash, but in the sense that we are manufacturing a product. There is no more important product that the human mind in shaping the future of our world. What successful manufacturing business has departments that barely work together in the production process and then assumes that the product will just assemble itself? Your students' brains are *your* product, your school is *your* business – there should be joined-up thinking across all departments, working together to create a whole child ready for a future we cannot yet envisage.

I left school a faulty product, managing to pass a handful of GCSEs but never feeling like I really understood what the whole experience had been about. Every lesson stood alone from the next, and only if I enjoyed the subject – if I 'got it' – did I pass the final exam. My poor maths teacher would regularly explode with hilarious pantomime displays of frustration as, once again I asked, 'But *when* am I ever going to use this, Sir?' I failed mathematics twice and only passed on the third attempt because I had decided that I wanted to go into teaching. Suddenly, there was a real reason to learn what my teacher had been trying to force into me for years. Unable to get onto the teaching course without a GCSE in maths, I knew I needed to pass this time. I had a reason to pass, and I did. If my teacher could have provided me with a valid reason to learn the first time around, if he had helped me to 'get it' and see some relevance in the hard work, I am sure I would have removed the pencils from my nose and passed first time.

Pupils experiencing the Manglish curriculum should feel that there is a point to everything they learn and that no new learning is left behind in an individual classroom, but is taken forward, used and improved. When these pupil-products are complete, no matter which road they take in life, they will have experienced an education that has taught them the importance of joined-up thinking. Pupils who spend their time asking, 'What's the point?' are not just looking to disrupt, they are searching for a 'Why?' Why are you making their head hurt with all of this difficult new information? Why should they keep listening when it is so difficult to grasp? A pupil experiencing the Manglish curriculum should be able to tell their teacher why. The perfect end product will not only be a knowledgeable pupil, but an individual who is able to practise their skills with autonomy. Autonomous pupils know that what they are learning is transferable and will be used as they journey through other lessons and through life. Rather than asking, 'What's the point?' the Manglish pupil will be bursting to tell you what they did with last week's mathematical learning in geography. Joined-up thinking will run through their veins.

A Manglish curriculum means that attainment will increase across the board, as literacy and numeracy underpin all learning. Pupils will be effective communicators, allowing them to participate in articulate debates in citizenship or group explorations in geography. Pupils will be skilled readers, allowing them to engage confidently with texts in science to explore evidence to support their choice of experiment. Pupils will be able to apply their mathematical skills in ICT when creating websites, using their knowledge of space and shape, and will write coherently in a range of contexts. Manglish will not only support pupils' achievement in English and maths to make the league tables look good, but it will create minds able to achieve across the curriculum.

The Manglish curriculum provides pupils with clarity and support, tailored to their individual needs. As they leave their primary experience behind and enter the world of secondary school, where each subject is separate and taught by different teachers, they are still able to feel that links between their learning experiences in one subject can explicitly relate to their experience in another. They will see that teachers are working together to support each other in the creation of the perfect final product, and no opportunities are missed and no child gets left behind. The Manglish child is not just a bag of bits – they are a complete and effective learner primed for a successful future.

Manglish and our future

Schools that adopt a Manglish approach will be at the forefront of education, producing perfect end products: pupils who are able to apply their knowledge and skills effectively beyond the classroom. Schools that wholeheartedly adopt a Manglish curriculum will develop the most skilled educators in the business: educators who are not blinkered by a subject-specific end-of-year exam but are working collaboratively to educate the minds of the future (after all, exam success comes naturally to pupils who see the point in learning). Teachers will remain subject specialists in their own right, while also understanding the importance of all subjects and their role in education as a whole.

The example Manglish curriculum presented to you in this book has been designed for a Year 7 cohort but this process will not end in Year 7. The model will be adapted and applied to all year groups as teachers continue to collaborate throughout pupils' education. Pupils will continue to purposefully apply reading, writing, communication and mathematics in all subjects as teachers identify, for themselves, the existing opportunities within their subject area. Manglish will become their state of mind and entire generations of pupils who understand the applicability of fundamental skills will be released into the real world. The problems associated with literacy and numeracy will no longer exist as pupils' education will be highly effective and applicable to their lives. I truly believe that this is possible if we make changes to the way we educate now. If we are all working together as educators of children, not as subject specialists in search of a final A–C pass mark, then we can achieve perfection in our end products.

The most successful candidates for any job are those who think in Manglish (even if they don't know it!). They are the people who see the point in connecting all skills and knowledge in order to create, innovate, lead and be led. This kind of person exists without the Manglish curriculum but they are not being purposefully created. The Manglish curriculum teaches all pupils how to achieve this state of mind as joined-up thinking and the wide application of skills becomes the standard. People with natural Manglish minds exist but are few and far between; this will remain the case if our education system remains as it is (a series of exam factories splurging out useless statistics).

'Remember this fact … write it in this order … this question should always be phrased like this … show your working for an extra point … never mind that you don't know why you are doing it, this formula will work … trust me, I know – I'm the specialist.' Much learning in schools today is not rooted in pupils' potential to use the skills learned beyond school, but is geared towards one end goal, the exam – resulting in future failure for the masses of pupils who don't 'get it'. Spoon-fed pupils regurgitate their teacher's words in tests (not really seeing the point other than the end grade). They may achieve a good result but will quickly forget their learning if they feel it is no longer needed. The end goal for most secondary teachers, through fear of their own failure, is another positive exam statistic for their school. This is not helping pupils to achieve in their future. This has to change.

A Manglish curriculum is the answer. I am not campaigning to scrap exams in favour of *Apprentice*-style end-of-year tests (although Project X does allow this to happen). Of course, there is merit in examining skills and knowledge but not if you are only doing it for an end grade and a statistic. I hope I have demonstrated how, by collaborating as educators in the business of creating a perfect end product – a pupil who thinks in Manglish – we can achieve the result of pupils who *can* and pupils who *do*. The examination years would still exist but, after three or so years of practising a Manglish curriculum, a pupil entering their examination years would be well aware of the purpose behind their learning. They would see a point in their maths exam, beyond the exam itself, and would also understand the purpose of learning in every subject. Examination results would naturally improve because pupils are now switched on to learning and its purpose in the world beyond the classroom.

There is nothing wrong with specialising. The world is diverse and we all have our own paths ahead of us, but it is wrong to be blinkered by our own subjects when developing a whole child. We are educators first and subject specialists second. As Peter Gloor, a researcher for Massachusetts Institute of Technology's Collaborative Innovation Networks says, 'Don't be a star; be a galaxy.'[2] Gloor believes that by working collaboratively as members of one world, we can solve the most difficult global problems. Similarly, by working together as educators, we can demonstrate to pupils the effectiveness of collaboration and the purposefulness of all learning beyond the immediate classroom they are in. They will leave school able to collaborate and solve problems that don't yet exist. We need to develop these great thinkers, now, before the problems arise. We will be ready.

The end ... or the beginning?

2   Peter Gloor is an MIT professor and is the chief creative officer and creator of the Galaxy Advisors team – this guy knows a thing or two about the impact that effective collaboration can have. His blog, *Communicate, Collaborate, Innovate*, is available at: <http://cci.mit.edu/pgloor/>.